# THE ROMANCE

~ OF ~

## BRITISH COLONIAL STYLE

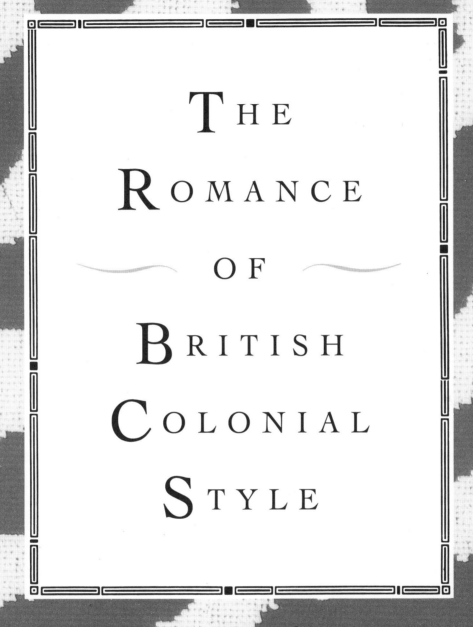

# The Romance

## of

## British

## Colonial

## Style

*Tricia Foley*

**Photographs by Jeff McNamara**

**Text by Catherine Calvert**

**Designed by Alexander Isley Design**

Clarkson Potter/Publishers, New York

Fabrics appearing on pages 1, 3, and 148 to 149 are from Clarence House Imports, Ltd.

Copyright © 1993 by Tricia Foley
Photographs copyright © 1993 by Jeff McNamara
Vintage photos reproduced by kind permission of the India Office Library

Published by Clarkson N. Potter, Inc., 201 East 50th Street, New York, New York 10022.
Member of the Crown Publishing Group.
Random House, Inc.   New York, Toronto, London, Sydney, Auckland

CLARKSON N. POTTER, POTTER, and colophon are trademarks of Clarkson N. Potter, Inc.
Manufactured in Japan
Design by Alexander Isley
Library of Congress Cataloging-in-Publication Data
Foley, Tricia.
The romance of British colonial style / Tricia Foley ; photographs by Jeff McNamara ; text by Catherine Calvert.
p.    cm.
Includes bibliographical references and index.
1. Interior decoration — Great Britain — Foreign influences.
2. Great Britain — Colonies — Social life and customs — Foreign influences.
I. McNamara, Jeff.   II. Calvert, Catherine.   III. Title.
NK2043.F66  1993
747.22′09′034 — dc20
92-30330
CIP
ISBN 0-517-58425-5
10  9  8  7  6  5  4  3  2  1
First Edition

# *Acknowledgments*

I would like to thank all those who helped this book come to life, especially

Jeff McNamara, who shared many adventures and trying times with me in

India and Africa; Catherine Calvert, whose way with words has evoked the

spirit of the Raj; Alex Isley, who designed the book; and Katherine Kali-

nowski, for all her patience and attention to detail. Many people here in New

York laid the groundwork for our journey: Pallavi Shah and Anita Trehan of

Our Personal Guest planned our exciting trip to all the outposts of the British

Empire in India and kept us on track through upsets and earthquakes. They also introduced us to many wonderful people who helped us along the way, including Glenn Dunmyre, David Gruber, Cynthia Polsky, Madhur Jaffrey, and Bal Mundkar, who arranged introductions for many of our finest locations. Manjit Kamdin, Robert Lighton of British Khaki, Burt Avedon and Susan Colby of Willis & Geiger, Michael Morelli of Ralph Lauren, and Charsi and Ian Harrington welcomed us into their homes and showrooms and allowed us to photograph their collections. Lynn Glenn of Into Africa led us to our Kenyan connections, and John Lampl and Lilla Santullo of British Airways graciously took care of all our flight arrangements to points east.

We will always remember Jackie McConnell of Robin Hurt Safaris, who led us on a house safari and shared her many experiences and good times with us in Kenya. Thanks to the Karen Blixen Museum and the Giraffe

Manor in Nairobi; the Mitchells of the Kiambethu Tea Farm; Donna Hurt of Wingu Kenda, Nicky and Michael Dyer of Burana; and those at the Mount Kenya Safari Club, the Aberdare Country Club, and Djinn Palace who so warmly welcomed us.

Many new friends in India took care of us on our trip. I am especially grateful to Deepak Talwar, Satish Kumar, and Sandip Singh of the Oberoi Grand in Calcutta for providing such an oasis for us. I would also like to thank the Tenduf La family at the Windamere Hotel in Darjeeling for their graciousness. Camellia Punjabi of the Taj Hotels, Vijay Katre of the Welcomgroup, and Peter Mahta and Rajiv Kaul of the Oberoi Hotels arranged wonderful accommodations for us.

Our thanks to the Tea Board of India and the Darjeeling Planters Association for their assistance with our research on this favorite topic of mine, and to our guides, Nandita Kathpalia in New Delhi and Mrs. Girija Duraiswami in Madras. Lady Mukherjee and the Burdwan family of Calcutta welcomed us into their homes, and we enjoyed our visits to the Royal Bombay Yacht Club, the Willingdon Club, the Asiatic Society, the Delhi Gymkhana, and the Ootacamund Club.

In London, Patricia Kattenhorn of the British Library, and the India Office Library and Records were very helpful in tracking down our images of the Raj period, and the St. James Court Hotel was home to us during our stay. To our "Safari on Long Island" crew, a great big thank-you to my family (especially Tom, Dennis, Mark, and Jim), Van Bankston, and Kathy Schmidt. I would also like to thank Regina McNamara for all her support throughout our project and Deborah Smith, Tom Johnson, and Colleen Rogan for their enthusiasm along the way.

Many, many thanks to my agents, Deborah Geltman and Gayle Benderoff, for their continued support and to Lauren Shakely, who guided us on our research for the legacy of the Empire. Our final thanks to Howard Klein, Nancy Maynes, Renato Stanisic, and all those at Clarkson Potter who made this book come true.

Tricia Foley
May 1993

# Contents

# *Preface*

Images of ceiling fans stirring lazily in the heat, wicker chairs nestled among palm trees, and striped shadows of light made by louvered doors have always appealed to me. Growing up on Long Island, far from England and its exotic colonies, I watched old movies set in the tropics with my father, read Somerset Maugham short stories like "The Letter," and bounced on my grandfather's knee as he recited "Gunga Din." More recently, I have been drawn to the nostalgic allure of movies like *Out of Africa* and *A Passage to India,* and the television series *Jewel in the Crown.*

Eventually, as the popularity of these productions continued — along with the popularity of safari jackets, beds draped with mosquito netting, and campaign furniture — I realized that I was not alone in my fascination with the British colonial period and its design heritage. Architecture, fashion, interior decoration, and cuisine around the world have all been influenced by the wonderful intermingling of English customs with those of the many cultures that were once part of the British Empire.

To capture the essence of that era, we "went out to the colonies" in search of bungalows and verandahs, steamer chairs and paisley shawls, the tea gardens of Darjeeling, the clubs of Calcutta, and the horse farms of Kenya. This book is a celebration of the romance and history of the British colonial style, which has endured long after the sun finally set on the British Empire.

Tricia Foley

May 1993

# Introduction

For more than three hundred years, England ruled an empire that encompassed, at its height, over a quarter of the earth's land and people. Beginning with the explorations of the East India Company in the early seventeenth century, the Empire expanded until the British ruled countries in nearly every corner of the globe. A schoolchild at the turn of the century studied a map of the world splashed with the pink tint that marked England's possessions, from small rocky islands off the coast of Africa to India and the entire continent of Australia. The British flag flew over steamy jungles and vast plains, trading posts and thriving seaports, over native peoples and expatriates who treasured their ties to England.

For generations of Englishmen and women, voyaging out to these distant lands and establishing government or trade was a life's work—a life's duty. Some joined the Army; some joined the Civil Service; others invested their own money in a plantation or a farm. They raised proper children, changed for dinner, drank tea at four o'clock, worshiped in steepled churches with Gothic windows—all the traditions of life at home. Yet they also developed their own special way of life, marked by insistence on form, nostalgia for home, and accommodation to the country in which they found themselves. Although there were minor variations from region to region by the time of the Empire's apogee, at the turn of the last century, the colonials around the world resembled one another more than they resem-

bled those they had left at home.

The British colonial style is closely linked to the lifestyles of settlers in India and, to a lesser extent, Africa. So long-lived, well-organized, and dominant was the British presence in India that Anglo-Indian slang, food, sport, and custom were exported throughout the Empire. The bungalow, for instance, the small house indigenous to India that was adopted and transformed by British settlers, was the model for housing from Australia to Africa; by the early part of this century the British were importing prefabricated bungalows to Africa as government-issued houses. Curry, an English invention (modified from Indian cuisine) and the centerpiece of Sunday lunch, was as likely to turn up in Kuala Lumpur as in Bombay. "The Empire builder's jargon would have filled a dictionary," commented Roald Dahl, who went to work in East Africa in the 1930s. "Much used words that seemed to be universal among all these people. An evening drink, for example, was always a sundowner. A drink at any other time was a chota peg. One's wife was the memsahib . . . supper was tiffin." This new language, adapted from Indian dialects, ultimately became the lingua franca of every British colony.

India was the model in home design as well. Dealing with a climate that was hotter and far more humid than that of home, the colonials turned to indigenous house styles for inspiration. Occasionally, there appeared a cottage seemingly imported brick by brick from Britain, down to the ivy trained to trail over the wall (Kenya's Happy Valley has quite a few examples of country cottage style), but most dwellings were low and breezy. Furnishings likewise reflected an adaptation to tropical climates; rooms were emptier, especially by Victorian standards, than those the settlers had left behind. Native materials like teak or bamboo were embraced, both for practicality and, in small doses, for novelty's sake.

By the height of colonization in the Victorian era, the English had been familiar with imports from the East — not only spices, but also porcelain, furnishings, and textiles — for more than two hundred years. Settlers arrived in the colonies already prizing some local production. Early settlers also

had the opportunity to observe the beautifully made furniture and lavishly appointed palaces of wealthy and educated Indians, and they bought or received as gifts similar household objects. When the English commissioned pieces from local craftsmen, the result was an amalgam of two cultures—a sofa with English Regency lines, a woven cane seat and back, and a curving leaf motif straight from a Moghul mosaic.

But local style and products never overwhelmed the essential Englishness of the household. "By dint of hanging up photographs, pictures, brackets for odds and ends of china, Japanese scrolls, having books and papers about, and a piano . . . a room can be made fairly pretty," advised one guide to living in the colonies. One of the principal roles of the Victorian wife was to ensure that, once a visitor crossed the threshold, he would imagine himself in Bath or Clapham. Even more than at home, the rules and customs of "civilized" behavior were followed as closely as possible.

The sun began to set on the British Empire nearly fifty years ago, with India's independence in 1947 and the gradual independence of the patchwork of protectorates and colonies. Yet, as Jan Morris wrote, "Empires come, empires go, and on the whole their intangibles last longest: manners, customs,

ways of thought, beliefs." Recently, there has been an increasing interest in the relics of Empire, whether literature, like Paul Scott's *The Raj Quartet* or Isak Dinesen's tales, or artifacts, like fine colonial furniture. Looking at how these colonials lived will inform us of the roots of many of the images we carry, a long moment of history now caught in amber, when the shadows crossed the verandah, the cane chairs creaked, and the ice clinked in the glass, a pause in the long twilight of a setting sun.

# GOING OUT

## *Tents, Trunks, and Teakettles*

**S**uddenly a puff of wind, a
puff faint and tepid and
laden with strange odours of
blossoms, of aromatic wood,
comes out of the still night —
the first sigh of the East on
my face. That I can never
forget. It was impalpable
and enslaving, like a charm,
like a whispered promise of
mysterious delight.

*Joseph Conrad*

# FOR SOME TRAVELERS,

the moment of arrival in India, Africa, Malaya, or one of the other far-flung points of debarkation in the Empire brought beauty, aroused their curiosity, and made them impatient to begin a new, more interesting life. For others, the novelty they faced was frightening, and the reality of their separation from family and friends was almost too painful to endure.

To ease reluctant passengers more gently into the unknowns of their future, elaborate preparations were made even before they boarded their boat. Passage by steamship lasted many weeks, and travelers needed to plan not only for the new life they were undertaking but also for the journey to it.

By the late nineteenth century, stores had been established throughout the colonies for shopping by mail or in person, but for generations colonials relied on the great London shops, such as the Army and Navy Stores, with their enormous illustrated catalogues and lists of requirements and necessities. One advertisement for "Messrs. Silver & Co., who know exactly what is needed for every part of the globe" promised tents with bathrooms as well as verandahs "as used by most eminent Travellers," fitted with a

OPPOSITE *Empire building required simple but well-equipped tents. Linens, mosquito netting, and a mirror made primitive quarters more civilized.*

full complement of folding furniture and watertight trunks. Tailors also adapted their goods for the new life: Burberrys made a sturdy cloth that withstood thornbush and monsoon, and soon the khaki suit and the bush shirt, with its military touches of flaps and buttons, became emblems of the Empire.

Possessions were divided into those stowed in the cabin, those consigned to the hold and inaccessible for the duration of the journey, labeled NOT WANTED ON VOYAGE, and trunks to which one could gain access once a day. The trunks were packed full — 335 pounds of clothes and equipment were permitted in the 1890s — and were often made in the East, lined with tin to protect clothing from insects. A typical outfit for a young cadet going to Africa in the 1920s included in its list of forty objects khaki ties and a wool bush shirt, leather leggings, a green canvas bucket, a folding chair of green canvas with leg rests, a compact chair bath and washstand that fit into a bag, a fitted cook's case, a steel helmet case, and two hurricane lamps; in addition there would be the tin boxes of food with which he was meant to sustain himself for

LEFT *The black umbrella became as familiar a sight in India as in London, here in Nilgiri.*

months. Victorian lady travelers had their own necessities (some boats were forced to ban hair curlers after shipboard fires), for the weeks were long and the formal occasions many as the boat made its way to Egypt and beyond.

From the mid-nineteenth century to the 1940s, most travelers going out to India booked passage on the P & O — Peninsular and Oriental — liners. In 1914, author Rumer Godden remembered, "The cabin was inviting with its white cotton counterpanes stamped

OPPOSITE *Wicker wrappings both insulated and protected bottles from breakage during a journey on rough roads; baskets of every kind transported movable feasts.*

ABOVE *Formal meals mimicked, as much as possible, the elaborate style of dinners back home — with an oriental carpet, potted palms, and cane chairs providing exotic touches. In 1904, the dining room of the Goorkha was ready for a seven course dinner.*

## ON SAFARI

In East Africa, leaving the settlements and touring the countryside was known as going on safari, from the Swahili word for "journey." (In West Africa such a trip was called "going to bush"; in Central Africa, *ulendo*.) Such safaris had many purposes, from the chores of administration — taking a tax census, inspecting crops, talking to villagers about their concerns — to the thrills of hunting game. All shared certain requirements, however, as every necessity of life, from vegetables to bathtubs, needed to be carried along. Dozens of porters and, later, trucks, carried canvas tents and folding chairs, cooking pots and mosquito netting for the impromptu villages that were raised along the way. With all the discomforts, travelers were also caught up in the romance of the trek — during which the porters sang as they walked or a district officer was welcomed with a feast or dancing — and they looked on these weeks as some of their best time in Africa.

with the letters P and O; a miniature mahogany and brass ladder was placed to lead up to the top bunk." Experienced travelers knew to escape the sun by booking cabins on the port side out, the starboard side home; their luggage markings, POSH, are said to be the origin of the term. In staterooms, dining rooms, cabins, and lounges, the ships were smaller versions of the colonies that awaited the passengers. Even at sea, planters separated themselves from Indian Civil Service officers, and missionaries kept apart from the rest. There were flirtations between bachelor officers and young women on their first solo visits to relatives, or even on their way to meet their fiancés. Lavish formal dinners and dances ended every day, and at night passengers strolled the decks, men in their handsome uniforms or in the white jacket and black trousers of

PRECEDING PAGES *By horse, by wagon, and, later, by car, colonists traveled simple roads in the hills of Kenya.*

ABOVE LEFT *The African plains were in stark contrast to the climate and geography of England.*

OPPOSITE *This steam engine still runs between Ootacamund and Coonoor in the south of India.*

Safaris — self-sufficient enterprises with dozens of bearers, servants, and equipment-laden pack animals — could travel long distances. Whether heading for the hills in India or crossing the African plains, travelers carried lightweight furniture, like the British canvas officers chairs, OPPOSITE ABOVE.

their clubs in Madras or Calcutta. Before the invention of the electric fan, passengers slept on deck too.

The usual route to India after the opening of the Suez Canal in 1869 was south along the coast of Europe, through the Strait of Gibraltar, across the Mediterranean Sea to Port Said in Egypt, through the canal to the Red Sea, around the horn of Africa to the Indian Ocean, and from there to Calcutta, Bombay, Madras, or a smaller port in India. (Ships bound for Kenya headed south along the coast after emerging from the canal.) It was said that the East began at Suez, and certainly the bright colors and new lan-

OPPOSITE In 1923, Lord Reading and his party picnicked in the Mysore forests of India.

LEFT AND ABOVE The utensils created by metalworkers of Mombasa in Africa were prized by colonials.

FOLLOWING PAGES Water-soaked wicker-covered bottles kept liquids cool.

guages, the jostling crowds and startling whitewashed buildings intrigued those who went ashore. Lady Canning, who traveled in some state in 1855 as the wife of the newly appointed Governor-General of India, wrote, "The first impression of the real East has an indescribable effect. Such extraordinary figures in various dresses, veiled women, strings of camels, and the buildings and strange southern vegetation make one feel in a dream." Later generations of travelers often bought their topees here, as they experienced their first taste of the southern sun.

Even when colonials had arrived at their destinations, traveling remained an important part of their lives, and households were organized to ensure portability. Governing the colonies meant touring the most out-of-the-way provincial stations to dispense justice or oversee construction projects. British administrators — few in number — ruled over thousands of miles, thousands of people, and they

LEFT *Cane and wicker chairs, folding tables, and sturdy baskets are as useful for picnics today as they were a hundred years ago.*

INSET LEFT *African wildlife is still the main attraction of the safari.*

constantly embarked on rounds of inspection. Planters often traveled back and forth to the city from their holdings hundreds of miles away; army families shifted with new assignments and duties.

Victorians were indefatigable travelers for pleasure and adventure, too, spending their holidays visiting places of beauty or historical interest, climbing mountains, or traveling by camel across the desert, sketchbook and diary close at hand. Going on safari, or to hunt, was a well-established custom in Africa and India. By the early nineteenth century in India, all who could afford it gathered up servants,

packing crates, and children and escaped to the foothills of the Himalayas to avoid the hot summer weather of the plains below. The hill stations of Simla, Ootacamund, and Kodaikanal, with their small bungalows clinging to the steep, pine-covered hillsides, became like little English villages, with church and graveyard, croquet grounds, and polo field. A proper move for a hill holiday in mid-Victorian times counted as necessities a bathtub, cooking pots, and twelve camel loads of furnishings.

Camps varied in appointments and formality. For a "trek" in Africa, each bearer carried about 56 pounds of

*Dansal camp paraphernalia*

OPPOSITE ABOVE
**P**lantations still terrace the hills
in India as they did one hundred
years ago.

ABOVE **I**n India, administrators
traveled in state throughout the
country for months at a time. This
expedition prepares to break camp
near Dansal in 1875.

LEFT **M**osquito netting and the
sola topee were essential to travel,
whether the accommodations were
tents, bungalows, or palaces.

gear and supplies. Camping equipment consisted of "a camp chair, a camp stool, a camp bed with a cork mattress and a tin bath with a cover and a wickerwork lining into which you packed all your toilet necessities," said one British traveler in a later reminiscence. In India, however, as Charles Allen commented, "touring was conducted on a far grander scale, in keeping with the Moghul tradition from which the custom descended." Sometimes travelers were quartered on other British residents for days, weeks, even months; the traditions of hospitality were preserved under all conditions. But the custom of touring with tents began with the earliest days of the Empire and continued to its end. Senior officials inspecting their territories required all the home comforts both for convenience and for impressing the princes and potentates they met along the way.

Emily Eden, who went out to India with her brother Lord Auckland in 1835, when he was named governor-general, spent as much as two years at a time traveling the length and breadth of his domain. Their train of servants, elephants, horses, and baggage carriers stretched for ten miles, stirring up dust that sifted into every bundle. The caravan boasted two sets of tents; one was sent ahead and pitched before their arrival each night

## THE SOLA TOPEE

For those accustomed to England's gray and rainy days, arrival in Africa or India meant exposure to a fierce and unfamiliar sun. Wide-brimmed hats sufficed to protect the earlier settlers, but by mid-Victorian times the *sola topee* or pith helmet (made of plant pith or pressed felt) had been developed to protect the wearer from the heat of the day. Stiff and bowl-shaped, the sola topee never collapsed, even under the hottest, most humid conditions, and allowed the scalp to "breathe" while reflecting the sun's rays. Women often further protected their backs with another layer of felt known as a "spine pad." From the time a child began to toddle about the garden, he or she wore a small sola topee, often trimmed with a ruffled muslin cover that tied under the chin. In time, these hats became the very symbol of the Empire and the English with it, with talismanic value to wearer and native alike. Until the adoption of the straw Panama hat (which came gradually and not until the twentieth century), no self-respecting Englishman went into the noonday sun without his sola topee.

OPPOSITE A *sola topee atop a wicker suitcase was a typical sight "east of the Suez." The Victorian rage for wicker found a special place in the British colonies, where the material suited the rigors of the climate.*

while the other was struck at the last camp. Although interiors were much simpler than those of later expeditions, they were still elaborate by modern camping standards: "Inside each tent were our beds—one leaf of a dining table and three cane chairs. Our *pittarahs* and the camel-trunks were brought in; and in about half an hour the *nazir* came to say all, with our books, dressing cases, & c., be carried off to be put under the care of a sentry, as nothing is safe." A dining tent and a durbar tent, for entertaining visiting rajahs, were also part of their encampment.

By mid-Victorian times, tents were as well furnished as any bungalow, with rugs and folding beds, traveling bookcases, and desks and drawered trunks, designed so that they could be set in place for immediate use.

Lessons learned from the portable furniture of both shipboard and soldiers' campaigns resulted in efficient and lightweight chests, tables, and chairs with seats of cane and canvas. Even palm trees were grown in pots, ready to move with the families. The letters of Lady Wilson, written

RIGHT *The British colonists perfected the art of enjoying meals out of doors, using local crafts along with their finest linens.*

## ~ STEAMER CHAIR ~

Well into this century, voyaging to the colonies meant a long sea trip, as carefully arranged and packed for as the ultimate destination itself. Boats became increasingly luxurious as the nineteenth century progressed, and shipboard rituals were established, from formal dinners to brisk walks round the deck. Hours were reserved, of course, for simply relaxing in a deck chair, moved into the sun or shade. Light, portable chairs were required, and some lines asked passengers to bring their own. A folding steamer chair was developed. It was substantial, with its wood frame, high back and leg rest, and broad, encompassing arms. A seat and back of woven cane kept passengers cool. Later, they accompanied the settlers to the verandahs of their new homes.

*Chairs of every conceivable kind could be found in colonial homes. The curved arms, heavy turned legs, and caned seat backs were hallmarks of the style, but every craftsman — from Bermuda to Bombay — interpreted the basic features differently.*

in 1889 as she traveled with her civil servant husband, give a good picture of camp life: "The string of 28 camels left an hour ago, with chairs, tables, and rolled-up tents roped on their backs, boxes filled with house-linen, dishes, silver, glass, pots and pans, clothes and books, fitting into huge paniers; and such an assortment as you never saw of hen coops, baths and every kind of incongruous extras piled on to their humps." Dogs, cats, sheep, cows, and extra horses followed along behind. Each night they pitched three tents—two for living in, one to serve as an office.

One night Lady Wilson wrote, "Anything cosier than our tent looks at this moment you could not imagine. We are sitting in our deck-chairs before the stove, with our feet on a wooden fender; the lamp behind us is hooked on to the central pole of the tent. Jim is reading the papers. . . . A bowlful of Gloire de Dijon roses on the table beside me is a delight to my eyes; beyond is a little bookcase filled with our favorite books, and on top of

it is the guitar. . . . We have pictures on our walls, comfortable chairs, tables and rugs."

The tents were about twenty feet square, with portions curtained off to serve as dressing rooms. A blue-striped dhurrie was spread over straw, and brass hooks held towels and dresses. Fifty men traveled with the Wilsons to attend to every need; the cook, carrying his own bright copper pots, created meals from local produce supplemented by tins of provisions from the Army and Navy Stores.

Other travelers chose to make their way from *dak* bungalow to *dak* bungalow; *daks* were government guest houses staffed by a few servants and appointed with simple furnishings. George Otto wrote a satirical play around 1863 called *The Dawk* [Dak]

OPPOSITE *The British stitched together the Empire with railways.*

RIGHT *A camp on the Guaso Nyiro shows the safari style of the turn of the century.*

DHARIWAL

DHARIWAL LONG LIFE WOOL WEAR
IS AS NECESSARY & AS WELCOME TO
INDIA AS SUNSHINE

FLANNELS,
VENETIAN CLOTHS,
BEAVERS,
MELTONS,
"DILARESCO"
SUITINGS,
WORSTEDS,
SERGES, TWEEDS,
BLANKETS,
RUGS, LOHIS,
BROADCLOTHS,
PUTTOOS,

ARMY GREATCOAT
CLOTHS,
UNIFORM CLOTHS,
PUTTIES,
SWEATERS,
JERSEYS, SOCKS,
UNDERWEAR,
BERLIN WOOL,
KNITTING AND
CARPET YARNS.

ABOVE "Kitting oneself out" —
buying all the necessities for life in
a new land — could be initiated in
London, but local purveyors knew
local needs.

RIGHT Large tents, gaily
decorated and hung with silks, are
of the Indian tradition for festivals
and special occasions.

OPPOSITE Wooden trader's
chests from Mombasa also served
as decorative furnishings in
colonial homes.

PRECEDING PAGES *By late in the last century, well-run trains covered the length and breadth of India.*

ABOVE *Intrepid women had joined their husbands as early as the sixteenth century. By 1896, they presided over the tea table (as here in Jaipur) just as their counterparts did back in England.*

OPPOSITE *Caned furniture had the "easy seat and springy back" (as one manufacturer put it) of upholstered furniture.*

*Bungalow, or Is His Appointment Pucka?* He introduced it: "This play takes its name from the comfortless hostelries of India, in which the larder consists of a live fowl, and the accommodation of three rooms on the ground floor, less than half furnished even according to Oriental notions of furniture; the traveler being supposed to bring with him bread, beer and bedding."

Amenities were indeed few, and each *dak* visitor was responsible for his own comforts, from the teapot to the tea to put into it. A traveler in the early nineteenth century cautioned about the food, "There was not much choice. A moorgee (fowl), or 'sudden

death' as they were called, was cooked either as a curry, grilled or roasted. This with rice kedgeree, a lentil condiment called dall, boiled eggs or an omelette, constituted a *dak* bungalow menu." A hundred years later another British visitor said, "When you arrived, you'd see your dinner scooting around the compound, then you'd hear it being caught, because there would be tremendous screeches. . . ."

Eventually, as the Raj reached its high point, a system of railways united the country, and families spent several days rocking on the rails, the windows of their cars often covered with slatted blinds and gauze to baffle the mosquitoes. Self-sufficiency remained the ideal, although a dining car served soup and roasts and puddings, and peddlers offered fresh fruit and hot tea at every station. The sahibs kept to their compartments, with their suitcases, hunting gear, and tiffin boxes.

In Africa, where British settlers were predominantly farmers rather than soldiers and civil servants, traveling was not just a way of life; it was an adventure. The safari, the African version of the hunting expedition, became a combination of a holiday and an athletic retreat. Women as well as men participated, in small groups led by native guides or professional British hunters, searching for game by day and playing cards around the campfire in the evening. Life in tents never quite reached the pinnacle of comfort in Africa, as it did in India, but safaris were well equipped, with lightweight, practical gear. Today's safaris arrive in the bush from the air, but they still offer the romantic sights and smells of colonial days.

ABOVE LEFT *Travel clocks like this one, with its well-worn braided leather strap, went from ship to safari, making sure that the schedule was kept.*

OPPOSITE *Reached by hours of travel on dusty roads, this farm, with its allee of trees, garden, and handsome bungalow, is like discovering a bit of England in Africa.*

# AT HOME

## *The Memsahib and Her Household*

We are but birds of
passage . . . and have to build
our nests of what material
we can find.

*Lady Wilson, 1889*

# THOSE WHO FIRST

voyaged to the colonies probably had little view to the future beyond making a fortune and returning to England, to live in comfort in the countryside, with a few pieces of Benares brass among the knickknacks or a watercolor of an African plain over the mantel. The early travelers were content to appropriate native style and native houses (and often, native

wives) for the few years they planned to stay, perhaps with the East India Company or sent by the church to convert the souls of the heathen. Planters and ranchers, who ventured far into the backcountry of India or the plains of Africa, found their lives very much interwoven with native culture.

The first settlers in the colonies were the traders dispatched by the East India Company, and the company administered much of the Empire through the nineteenth century, ceding control to the British government after the Indian mutiny of 1859. The British settled in East Africa much later: the British East Africa Company was founded in 1888, and the first settler in Kenya did not arrive until 1903.

The women who bravely accompanied their men in the early years were sometimes more adventurous

OPPOSITE *A chair caned in a particularly handsome pattern, a coir carpet, and a folding drinks tray are trademarks of colonial style.*

## COIR AND SISAL

In tropical climates, wool carpets quickly fell victim to climate and insects. Even if they could be preserved, they were impractical, since they were designed to retain heat. To cover cool tile or wood floors, colonials looked to local products for inspiration and adopted the inexpensive and readily obtainable woven mats they discovered there. Coir, woven of fibers extracted from coconut husks, and sisal, made from the sisal plant, provided attractive and practical rugs.

India remains the world's primary source for coir. The production of coir is still a handcraft passed down through the generations; some half million people are employed in this craft. Over the centuries techniques for preparing the coconut husk, beating the fiber into malleability, drying the fiber, and spinning it into yarn have changed very little. Coir yarn is used for mats, carpets, and rope.

ABOVE RIGHT *A coir runner protects the mahogany stairs of a home in India.*

BELOW RIGHT *An etched glass hurricane shade was both decorative and useful for breezy evenings on the verandah.*

OPPOSITE *Banana leaves in a brass container grace an elegant stairway landing in Karen, Kenya.*

than those who were the backbone of the Empire in the mid-Victorian era and later. There was room for the lady who rode astride and loosened her stays, who ventured among the native people out of curiosity or conviction. There were fewer conventions to be flouted, and less state to be maintained. But most colonial women still pursued their watercolors and their afternoon naps.

By the mid–nineteenth century, much had changed in style and attitudes, both in Britain and abroad. The home became a sacred spot, the wife its priestess, with no higher endeavor than tending her children and decorating her house. To her fell the formidable task of establishing a bastion of propriety in the wilderness. Through monsoon and drought, women survived by sheer determination, energy, and regular doses of quinine. They maintained the image of the British home, usually commanding battalions of servants, and went about their rounds with the ceremony and pomp of the queen herself.

The first Western-style building erected in the community was usually the church, which might resemble its steepled brother back in England and was soon surrounded by a rapidly filling graveyard, as the settlers succumbed to virulent new diseases, often compounded by melancholy.

OPPOSITE *A parasol and a straw picture hat were essential for shielding delicate complexions from the sun.*

ABOVE *Flower gardens were precious to colonial wives, who prized new varieties but made room for lilies and lupins from home.*

OPPOSITE *This contemporary living room has elements of colonial style — a cashmere shawl, coir rug, and club chair with khaki upholstery fabric.*

ABOVE *The bungalow, whose design derived from indigenous, simple one-story houses with broad verandahs, spread throughout the Empire.*

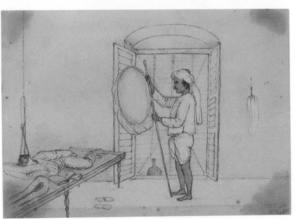

*Nineteenth-century sketches capture typical scenes from Anglo-Indian life:*
TOP *A servant operates a punkah from an adjacent room;*
ABOVE *A servant fans a man taking a nap on a day bed called a charpoy;*
LEFT *A woman sits beneath a punkah, a calico-draped fan. A curtain at the door offers privacy in the busy household without forfeiting breezes.*

Settlements in Africa and beyond remained small for the most part, but the English presence in India soon required extensive building as wealth began to pour out of the country and more English arrived to administer the colony.

After the Sepoy Mutiny of 1858, when Indian troops massacred hundreds of British soldiers, women, and children, the British withdrew from the strange and frightening world around them, creating a society within a society. A bride joining her army husband in the colonies in 1920 knew a world very similar to that her mother or grandmother had known in Victorian or Edwardian England. Unless the posting was to a large city, like Calcutta or Bombay, English life revolved around the cantonments, descendants of army camps that served as centers for the military and civil-

PRECEDING PAGES *Bedrooms in Nairobi* (LEFT) *and Bombay* (RIGHT) *show elements common to homes around the Empire.*

ABOVE RIGHT *A shaving mirror was a necessity in a dressing room or in camp.*

OPPOSITE *The walls of a bedroom are hung with a tent of navy-and-white-striped canvas.*

ians alike. There would be a noisy bazaar of swirling crowds and stalls selling chickens or saris, then the broad, green stretch of lawn known as the *maidan*, which might serve as promenade or parade ground. Then came the military headquarters, barracks, and houses for troops and some families; this was followed by the "civil line," where civil servants and tradespeople lived, interspersed with a club and a church, a park or two, some shops, and tennis courts. "Most of the houses were one-storeyed, with flat roofs and thatched verandahs. . . . There were *kutcha* [raw, unfinished] bungalows, also, buildings of timber and bamboo matting with thatched

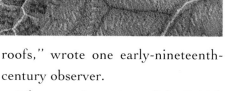

roofs," wrote one early-nineteenth-century observer.

Like many inventions of the British colonial era, the bungalow has mysterious origins, although most agree the style derives from Indian models. Historian Charles Allen quoted an Anglo-Indian glossary defining a bungalow as a building "of one storey and covered by a pyramidal roof, which in the normal bungalow is of thatch but may be of tiles. In both name and form it has its origins in the old Hindu kingdom of Bangala."

This rudimentary structure, the colonial equivalent of a cottage, rested on a low brick platform and was often topped with a peaked thatch roof. During the era of Romanticism in the early nineteenth century, when the notion of an idyllic pastoral life gripped Europe, many arriving English brought a vision of a picturesque villa that they adapted to the realities of colonial life. They embraced practical and exotic elements of local architecture — the wide verandah, which sheltered against both monsoon and scorching sun, and the open plan, which permitted breezes to flow from one end of the house to the other.

This simple house soon became universal in the colonies, from Australia to South Africa (and even back in England), with variations often determined by differences in location and climate. Through the years, the architectural flourishes of changing tastes at home were grafted onto the simple form — Gothic castellations and peaked windows, Doric columns when Neoclassical details were popular, and, finally, the carpentered fancywork that has come to be identified with Victorian architecture around the world. Bungalows could be grand,

OPPOSITE LEFT *Traditional crewel embroidery graces this Kashmiri shawl.*

OPPOSITE RIGHT *Early sketches of exotic flora were in turn popularized through botanical prints.*

ABOVE RIGHT *The tea plant bears delicate white flowers.*

## TEA

Tea drinking began in China, but enterprising traders brought the leaf to Europe by the late seventeenth century, and drinking the brew became an established part of the English day. Tea grew wild in India, and in 1841 a Scot imported tea plants from China to the outskirts of Darjeeling. His success encouraged other planters, and hopeful investors established plantations throughout the country. By 1888 more tea was imported to England from Darjeeling, Assam, and Nilgiri than from China.

Even in the hot climate of Africa or the Indian plains, colonials sipped their tea, from the first cup brought to their rooms as they rose from bed to teatime in the late afternoon. Although tea cultivation began in India, the English imported the rituals of tea drinking (one lump or two?) to the colonies. As in England, tea served as a vehicle for entertaining, whether at home, for a garden fête, or at a gymkhana gathering.

covered with highly polished *chunam* (a kind of stucco made of ground seashells); Madras, with its rows of white houses, reminded a visitor in 1781 "of a Grecian city in the age of Alexander."

Although humble bungalows were surrounded by a bit of beaten earth and a straggling bush or two, more established bungalows boasted large gardens. Much of the ground was required for domestic offices, because the platoons of servants did not live in the house, but established their own dwelling places nearby, strictly segregated by caste and religion. There was likely to be a water tank, a cow, and then flower gardens that were a riot of color and scent.

Rumer Godden remembered the first sight of her family's house in Bengal after five years spent in England. After passing the gatehouse

ABOVE LEFT *Sturdy luggage with reinforced metal corners once accompanied colonists on their voyages.*

OPPOSITE *A Sri Lankan tall, posted mahogany bed displays a Dutch influence in its carving.*

BELOW LEFT *Picture frames crowd tables and mantles, as in this home in Kenya.*

and entering the gravel drive, they passed a tree that "burst into a tent of white blossom and had round its foot a bed of amaryllis lilies with red streaked trumpets. Lawns . . . of unbelievable magnitude spread away on either side after the strip of London garden we had grown used to. . . . We saw roses and sweetpeas, and flowers we had forgotten, hibiscus and oleanders. Magenta bougainvilleas climbed to the top of tall trees," with a hedge of poinsettias and pots of chrysanthemums marching up the steps.

Surrounded by so much that was wild and unknown, colonial women took seriously their duty to tame the small acreage at their command. Garden planning and supervision were important, and arranging the cut flowers for her house was one of the duties never delegated to a servant. In the cooler hill stations, where families retreated during the hottest months, bungalow gardens recalled the finest

PRECEDING PAGES *A contemporary American study displays fine pieces from colonial Sri Lanka, once Ceylon.*

ABOVE *Silver flatware with mother of pearl handles was especially popular with the colonists.*

OPPOSITE *The home of Karen Blixen — the author "Isak Dinesen" — outside Nairobi, is now a museum.*

ABOVE **K**ashmiri shawls were
prized by Victorian ladies around
the world.

TOP RIGHT **B**ungalows could be
simple in style or as grand as
mansions, as this double-
verandahed house in Rangoon,
Burma, about 1890.

CENTER RIGHT **A** summer
bungalow in India displays a taste
for fretwork.

RIGHT **T**eak Sri Lankan
furniture is at home in a Long
Island garden.

*The mahogany plantation chair is backed with cane and pillowed in canvas. The lines of the chair and its matching ottoman are reinterpretations of British Regency style.*

## PAISLEY

The pattern we know as paisley, named after a small Scottish city famous for its weaving, in fact had its origins in Kashmir, where woven mantles were worn by men at the Moghul Court of the sixteenth century. Called by the Persian word *shawl,* lengths of material made of this fabric were woven of fine goat hair and were notable for their elaborate designs, full or intricate lacings of flowers. As time passed, the flower designs were refined into a stylized, teardrop-shaped bouquet dubbed a *buta* (pinecone), which soon became the identifying design we call paisley. The shawls, imported to Europe, became a mainstay of fashion from the late eighteenth to the nineteenth centuries and were copied by manufacturers in Norwich, England, and Edinburgh and Paisley, Scotland.

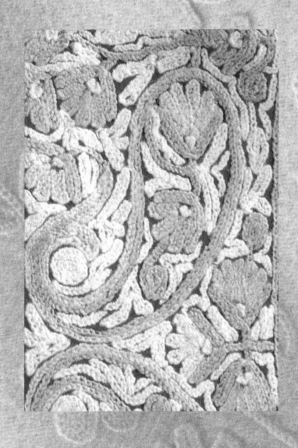

## VERANDAH

A distinctive feature of colonial architecture in warm climates is the verandah, a colonnaded porch, grand or humble, that was the favorite spot to enjoy a breeze while retreating from the sun. Hung with muslin or grass mats in the early days, verandahs ultimately became small drawing rooms, centers for family life and informal entertaining. Heat was tempered by *tatis* — woven grass mats, soaked with cool water in the morning — or by latticework or louvered blinds. Here potted plants were nurtured and birdcages were hung in the shade. Furnished with rattan or cane tables and chairs, especially lounge chairs, the verandah was the most comfortable "room" in the house. Even more desirable than one verandah was two, at both the ground and second-story levels.

cottage gardens of Britain, with colorful masses of perennials.

Whether highborn ladies or soldiers' wives, most women traveled out with the essentials for housekeeping and a few luxuries. As more wives journeyed to the colonies, guides, cookbooks, and housekeeping manuals proliferated to introduce them to the world they were entering. Most advised the traveler to bring little furniture, because constant moves would destroy it. (One Victorian advisor cautioned that footstools were useful to keep one's feet away from scorpions and centipedes.) There was room in the baggage for household linen, pictures, and books; for the wardrobe that would encompass tennis party, hunt ball, and jungle travel; and for a number of the knickknacks — photographs, bits of china — that Victorian taste demanded and that were essential to travelers as powerful reminders of home.

All the other aspects of the bungalow were in marked contrast to the

ABOVE LEFT *The verandah, shown here in a late nineteenth-century photograph, served as an outdoor parlor.*

OPPOSITE *Long flat arms and a sloping back are distinctive features of the planter's chair.*

draperies and overstuffed furniture, the patterned wallpapers, and the woolen carpeting that epitomized the English ideal of home. In India, "the ceilings were high, with rough, uncovered beams. . . . the walls were whitewashed, because wallpaper was merely a temptation to white ants. The floors were often beaten mud (since termites loved wood), covered with grass or bamboo matting. Lighting all this, at least until electricity spread in the twentieth century, were candles or paraffin and coconut-oil lamps. The general effect was of a gloomy austerity," wrote historian Margaret MacMillan, whose family served in the Raj.

Climate prompted many domestic adaptations. "It is so very HOT I do not know how to spell it large enough," wrote Emily Eden in 1835. Ice was imported to India from New England by a clever entrepreneur in 1840, and the electric fan arrived almost a century later, but for the most part settlers had to make do with the colonies as they found them. In addition to verandahs and *jhilmils,* or local venetian blinds, every room in India had, hanging from the ceiling, a punkah, a large, oblong, rigid fan draped in muslin, pulled from the hallway with a long rope by a punkah wallah. "It was like a set of large lady's drawers waving over one's head," said one

PRECEDING PAGES *A Sri Lankan chest is the centerpiece of this American library.*

OPPOSITE *Karen Blixen brought her furniture as part of her dowry from Denmark to her coffee plantation in Kenya in 1914.*

ABOVE *Blixen spent her days on horseback running the farm; her gear is draped on a chair.*

resident, and even Lady Canning, the model of Victorian rectitude and forbearance, complained, "The fuss of punkahs was wholly unnecessary, but there they were going like mad!" She felt sorry, too, for the punkah wallah, forced to tug his rope all night, but she succumbed to the pleasure of a breeze in the depths of summer.

Rooms had many doors to the verandahs and to one another, encourag-

PRECEDING PAGES *Potted palms, shutters, and dark woodwork create a colonial mood in a New York apartment.*

ABOVE *Blixen's farmhouse is stone with a tile roof.*

OPPOSITE *The rear verandah of Blixen's farmhouse offered respite from the heat of the African plains.*

ABOVE *The verandah was treated as an extra room, where Blixen and her guests could eat or work and enjoy the view of the Ngong Hills in the distance.*

ing cross ventilation, and the English felt the loss of privacy almost as keenly as the heat. As the sun grew hotter, large grass screens called *tatis* were wet, then placed around each porch and balcony, casting the interior into darkness until evening, when windows were thrown open, the earth cooled, breezes stirred, and life took on a faster pace. Well into the Victorian era, a lady spent the midday resting, sketching, and recording her day in her diary. She attended to the household and its chores in the morning and spent her evenings riding or paying calls in the carriage. When the Victorian spirit for improving each shining hour took hold, some of the memsahibs became less languid. By this century, a new emphasis on sport and a new ease of dress allowed them more activity, with tennis and riding at the club often women's main focus.

Setting up house, however, preoc-

TOP LEFT *The gramophone that Denys Finch Hatton brought to Karen Blixen is still kept at her home in Nairobi.*

LEFT *Victorian gardeners prized the luxuriant roses they were able to grow in exotic climates.*

OPPOSITE *Blixen loved the cuckoo clock in her library.*

cupied most women's days. Eventually, a style of decor evolved that was a mix of nostalgia for Britain and colonial practicality. The first impulse was undoubtedly to replicate home, whether it was a castle or a cottage. The colonial wife was likely to rent furniture, or to commission it from a local carpenter. Violet Jacob, whose army officer husband served in the plains of Central India in the 1890s, wrote of having a sofa made to order: "We wanted a long bamboo sofa made for one of the rooms and told Soloman to get someone to do it." Two days later, the sofa appeared, a triumph of bamboo and cane.

British colonial furniture may have had its design antecedents in London,

*TOP LEFT The home of Colonel Keyes in Abbottabad, photographed in 1865, was in the bungalow style so popular among colonists throughout the empire.*

*CENTER LEFT Camping in the 1870s in the Bombay state meant a tent community with room for pets and such amenities as the local woven cotton dhurrie rug.*

*BOTTOM LEFT In Jaipur, a well-turned-out carriage awaits its passengers before a thatched-roofed bungalow.*

*OPPOSITE A nap during the heat of midday was a necessity; men returned to work after stretching out on a caned daybed like this one from Sri Lanka.*

but its materials were strictly Indian. There were new and exotic woods — rosewood, teak, camphorwood, mahogany, and the inexpensive and easily transportable bamboo. Foiling the local insect life, too, required careful choice of materials; upholstery, likely to be a haven for white ants and worse, had to be forgone in favor of cane, a handsome alternative with easily replaceable cushions. (Emily Eden had her usual tart comment on the insect life: "The degree of destructiveness of this climate it is impossible to calculate, but there is something ingenious in the manner in which the climate and the insects contrive to divide the work. One cracks the bindings of the books, the other eats up the inside; the damp turns the satin gown itself yellow, and the cockroaches eat up the net that trims it; the heat splits the ivory of a miniature, and the white maggots eat the paint; and so they go on helping each other and never missing anything.")

Designs, too, never completely replicated those of home; an Indian craftsman added his own flourishes to

*RIGHT* **T**he *sconces that illuminate this American living room were common in colonial days, lighted then by oil or candle. Palms, linen, and cashmere throws recall the days of the Raj.*

the carving required on a George IV rosewood side chair, incorporating motifs with which he was familiar, such as leaves, fluted columns, or scroll backs. And, with the slow communication from home and the basic conservatism of the colonists, the major style trends from Europe overtook India much more slowly and remained popular longer.

ABOVE *Blinds and shutters were necessary at every window to block the sun, afford privacy, and permit breezes.*

OPPOSITE *An Anglo-Indian bed displays the bolder turnings and heavier lines that mark colonial furniture.*

Since the heat forced so much languor, seating predominated among the furnishings. Edith Cuthell, who knew India before the First World War, said it was "the land of loll. There are chairs for each sex and size — long bamboo couch chairs; small grass chairs, cretonne-clad, corresponding to wicker ones in England; heavy dark teak, or mahogany chairs, with wide cane seats and tall curling backs, monsters, with great flat wooden arms splayed out to receive the Sahib's extended legs."

Colonists soon developed a taste for some indigenous crafts, such as dhurrie rugs and Benares brass, which, used sparingly, added an essential exotic note. Isabel Savory, at the end of the nineteenth century, described a

OPPOSITE *Karen Blixen's pitcher and wash basin display her Scandinavian taste for simplicity and soft light colors.*

typical bungalow interior: "The rooms are invariably dark, and almost bristle with a hundred . . . little Indian, Kashmir and Burmese tables, stools and screens." Mounted animal heads or an elephant's foot umbrella stand marked the residence of a family who enjoyed hunting. There were precious objects, too, for those who could afford them, ivories and silks and painted miniatures; the favorite treasures of the rajahs became prized by their rulers as well.

At the grand end of the scale, the effect could be as impressive as that of any palace. Lady Canning worked hard arranging her enormous sitting room — it had thirteen doors and three windows — at Government House, Barrackpore, and she painted a picture of it in its finished state. "I am getting so fond of this place. I believe

ABOVE LEFT *An antique wool shawl, now in an Indian collection, would have been a prized possession in colonial India.*

BELOW LEFT *New York Safari outfitters Willis & Geiger have been supplying travelers with camping gear for over a hundred years. Clark Gable, Grace Kelly, and Amelia Earhart all set out for adventure clothed in outfits from this venerable firm.*

largely makeshift. . . . There was a wide fireseat and in front of it a brass tea-table on which brass elephants marched holding up a brass kettle on their brass trunks; Aunt Mary had won it in a tennis tournament. The tea caddy was tortoiseshell and very old; it stood . . . with the Crown Derby cups and a tiny Dresden cup. . . . Half of the double room was left almost bare, holding only the upright piano and the music rack. . . . There was a sofa and a bearskin with a snarling stuffed head."

Her house arranged, her servants organized, the memsahib had the day,

it would look rather nice even as an English country-house, so marvellously is it improved by 450 yards of rose-chintz, a great many arm-chairs, small round tables, framed drawings etc., and flowerpots in number." Formerly lady-in-waiting to Queen Victoria, Lady Canning had brought with her portraits of the royal family to brighten the walls.

Even Rumer Godden's middle-class family had created an inviting drawing room, using precious heirlooms from England and Indian originals. "To us the drawing-room was a beautiful room though its furniture was

ABOVE LEFT *An early print illustrates elements of colonial style: dhurrie rugs, louvered doors, roll-up blinds.*

ABOVE *Trophies of the hunt were popular; here, a crocodile notebook cover.*

OPPOSITE *Reeds, wicker, and sweet grass were woven into these suitcases and hampers.*

the week, the years to fill as she chose. It took discipline not to fall into idleness. Lady Canning wrote: "It is provoking to feel so utterly useless . . . but I should like to be good for something. My personal life is uneventful. Putting dimity in a drawing room or a new mat, is about the principal event I can look forward to: or choosing 30 names out of a list for dinner . . . three times a week." She, as the wife of the governor-general, had a ceremonial function to fulfill; the ordinary wife followed some of the same rituals, but on a smaller scale.

Women who felt a strong sense of duty turned to charity work. Philip Mason recalled one "formidable old lady . . . who after her morning ride and her inspection of the stables and the garden, the cook-house and the cook, would then be off to her maternity center and child welfare clinic in the city and would fit in a purdah party (women only) for Indian ladies before her dinner party for the brigadier. She told the cook exactly what to do; she saw that his pans were properly scoured and the kitchen

*RIGHT Photographic portraits of family members back in England dominated the décor of many sitting rooms, assembled among more exotic trophies — Indian swords and animal skins.*

table scrubbed; she inspected the dishcloths . . . she really was the platonic ideal of the memsahib." Most British children were sent home for schooling by their fifth year (handsomely framed photographs and

ABOVE *The ivory escutcheons on this 1810 English mahogany chest were probably imported from India.*

OPPOSITE *Touches of colonial style in an American bedroom include paisley on a stool and a miniature campaign chest.*

paintings of those faraway children held pride of place in most sitting rooms), for it was thought the ayahs (Indian nurses) would spoil them. Social life became all-important, and long after those back in England had loosened some of their social strictures (in fact, until the end of the Raj in 1947), the colonials honored the art of the calling card and the importance of the dinner jacket, and their hospitality was legendary.

It was obligatory to set a handsome table. The day began with *chota hazri*, early tea, served in the bedroom. In

the high Victorian era breakfast, served in the dining room, could be a multicourse feast, with everything from fried fish to chops. Well into this century, the breakfast table served hearty appetites with a cross of cultures: there would be eggs and bacon and hot buttered toast, but also yoghurt and warm *chapattis* (soft fried bread), and a spicy omelette might appear as well. A favorite everywhere was kedgeree, a scrambled dish of boiled rice, smoked fish, boiled eggs, herbs, and lots of butter.

Tiffin, the noontime meal, might bring a husband home from the office (although many stopped for a pink gin at the club on the way) or, on the weekend, guests for a curry and lots of rice. Even with silver salvers and cut-glass dishes of relishes, tiffin was a simple meal compared with the formal dinners at night, and it might be packed up for a picnic in the hills or carried outside to the verandah. A few

OPPOSITE **N**o *lady in Victorian times ventured forth without her parasol; even in Africa or India she worked to preserve her English rose complexion.*

ABOVE RIGHT **A** *traveling cup, which could be collapsed and tucked into a leather case, was a keepsake when worked in silver.*

hours later tea was served, either as a family meal with doily-covered plates of sandwiches or in the large ceremonial garden parties that, for instance, marked a royal birthday. Official celebrations, given by a governor or a ranking officer, were attended by all members of the community in their best hats, uniforms, and silk dresses.

Tea also concluded a tennis tour-

nament or a charity fête, and local cooks in Kenya and in India became accomplished at cutting the crusts from cucumber sandwiches and serving up curry puffs. The eighteenth-century English had eaten their largest meal of the day in the early afternoon; the Victorians and Edwardians brought the dinner party into prominence. Especially in India, the dinner party honored social hierarchies and proper form. The Warrant of Precedence, organized and then expanded throughout the nineteenth century, identified the particulars of each rank of the Civil Service, amounting, in 1947, to sixty-one levels; among them, the chief justice of Bengal was number 7, and the political secretary, number 47. With a copy of the warrant in hand, the hostess could issue her invitations properly and seat her tables accurately.

Dinner was elaborately presented on long, polished mahogany tables,

OPPOSITE *The discovery of the bazaar and its treasures delighted many a newcomer to India, who collected ivory and glass beads and bangles (Hindi for bracelet).*

ABOVE RIGHT *A tea caddy dating from the beginnings of the tea trade in India has a carved snake motif on its lid.*

with family silver and starched linens. Jennifer Brennan, from a family of several generations' residence in India, remembered the dinner parties her grandparents gave in the early 1920s: "It was a menu order that lasted in India right up to the disappearance of the British Raj. There was a first toast, which consisted of a small preparation on fried bread. Following that was soup, then fish, entree (some rather complex dish . . . ), the main dish—a roast, pudding . . . and then 'seconds' or 'siccuns,' as the Indians called them. There were always fruit and nuts, and little *bowli* glasses or bowls of scented water with rose petals in them to wash one's fingers. There were silver or crystal dishes of fudge and other sweetmeats on the table, and then the port and madeira would be brought round."

To do justice to such a meal, gentlemen arrived in white or black tie, their ladies in glittering evening gowns (augmented, when they sat at table, by pillowcases drawn over their legs to protect them from mosquitoes). Whether dining on safari on the remotest of African plains, on a journey through a jungle, or at home in Bombay, the English infallibly dressed for dinner. Anything less would have been letting the side down. One Victorian colonial guidebook intoned, "We would inveigh against any yielding to the lassitude and indifference which comes over the most energetic in tropical heat." For generations of women in the colonies, such solemn proscriptions governed not only the dinner party but also their entire existence.

RIGHT **A** *New York City living room recalls the traditions of the colonies, in its coir rugs, palms, and draped shawl.*

# THE CLUB

*Polo in
the Morning,
a Drink
at Sundown*

**The Club! Oh, the Club! I
never would have lasted if it
hadn't been for the Club.**
*A retired major*

# IT HAS BEEN SAID

that no sooner do two or three Englishmen meet than they decide to form a club. Perhaps nowhere was the club more central to British life than in the colonies, where it formed not just one of many diversions but often the only source of social activity for the English community. In the first period of settlement, in the mid–nineteenth century, work was

hard, days were long, men lived without women in small settlements or isolated in the backcountry, and social encounters revolved around the drinks tray and the polo field. The club followed shortly thereafter, already in place to welcome the arrival of women and families, and the other elements of a civilized life.

In England, particularly in London, during Queen Victoria's time, club life was the center of a gentleman's day. Begun in the eighteenth century, when informal gatherings at coffee houses evolved into the grand men's institutions of Pall Mall and Saint James's, clubs became essential to middle- and upper-class life of the Victorian period. In them, protected from the demands of wife, children, and household, a man collected his mail, took his lunch, drowsed in the library, and settled political questions over the billiards table. When his fam-

OPPOSITE **"Snooty Ooty,"** *the 150-year-old Ootacamund Club (see preceding pages) sponsored sporting events; winners, long vanished, live on in the gilt-lettered notices.*

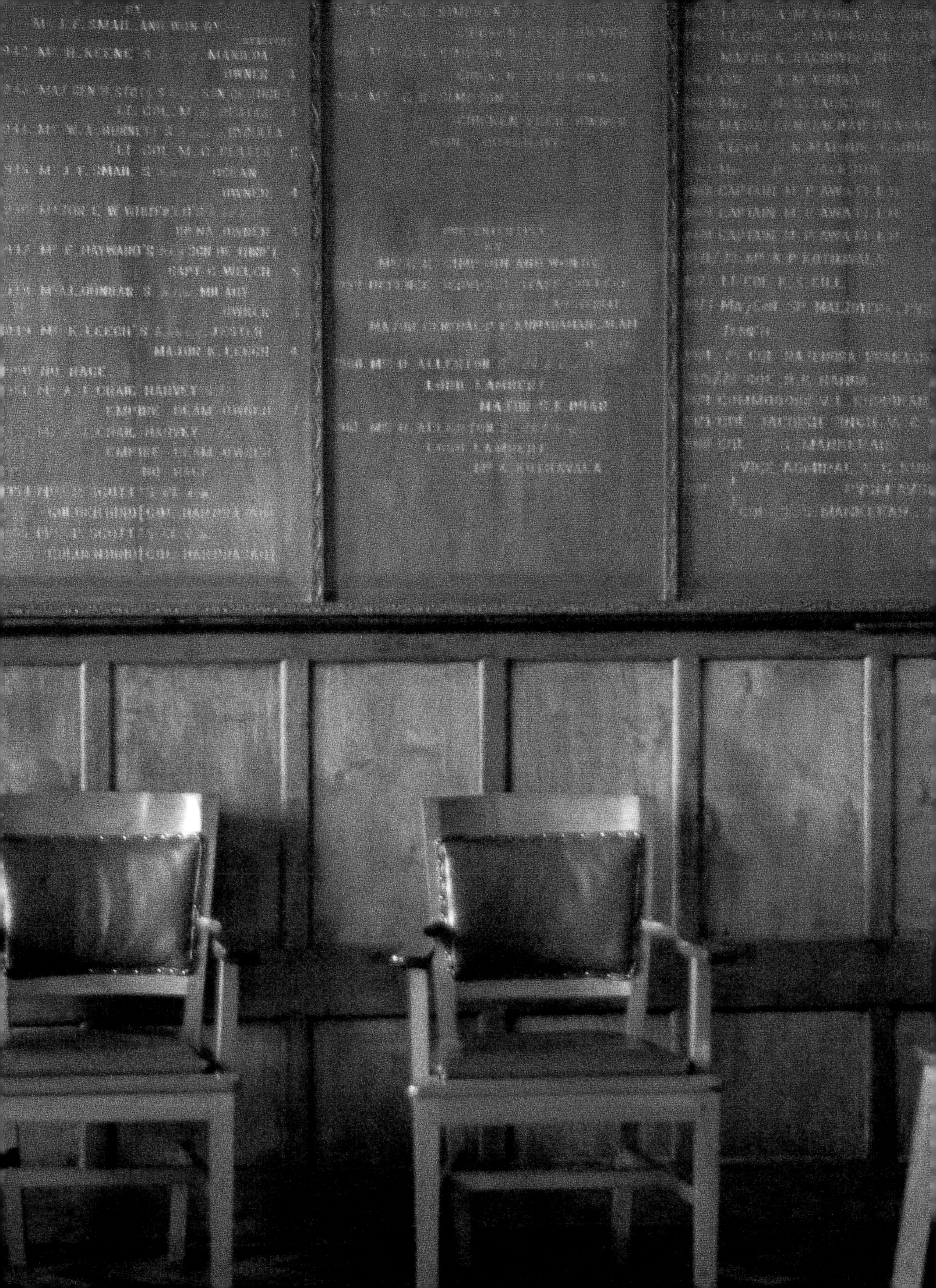

mess became the gathering place for the military in the colonies, followed by the civilian equivalent in the form of a variety of clubs. The typical men's club attempted to replicate the aura of its cousins back in England. Although in India the climate rendered ceiling fans an essential feature and the leather-bound books fell victim to silverfish and mildew in a season, there were still the traditional leather-covered club chairs, a selection of newspapers, and a drinks tray with cut-crystal tumblers. The most prestigious of these establishments was the Madras Club, founded in 1831. With the arrival of women and families, de-

ily took to the country for a long holiday and work demanded his presence in town, the club served as a hotel. Here careers were launched and networks established for a lifetime of fraternal support and congeniality.

As the Empire grew, the officers'

OPPOSITE *Victoria still reigns over the Ooty Club, where members retired to study a week-old newspaper, or to nap in the heat of the day.*

ABOVE *The mess rooms of the Wiltshire Regiment were a men-only world filled with ceremony.*

RIGHT *The Bombay Yacht Club was built in 1846, in neoclassical style. Doors open from the verandah to the meeting rooms.*

*1883*

Burrows Collector of Nilgiris · Col Ben Symons master · Col Tillard Bains · 2 Hamlin Col Robert · Gen R Stewart · S Orr · C Campbell

mand for sporting clubs — with stables and tennis courts — increased. The source of lessons and tournaments during the day, the club became at night the site of fancy balls, where couples danced the waltz, turkey trot, and reel.

"A lot of fun has been poked at club life in India," wrote a British resident there in the 1930s, "without those who indulged in this sort of sport realizing how vital a part of the life it

ABOVE **M***embers of the Ootacamund Club gather before a hunt at the turn of the century. Trophies and old photographs like this one line the club's halls.*

OPPOSITE **H***andsome trophy cases display models of winning yachts from the past at the Bombay Yacht Club. The club still serves as a social center as well as a sailors' refuge.*

was. Getting together for games and exercise and talk was really a very important part of our life. It was the social center of the civil and military station." The same was true in Africa, where in the larger stations residents enjoyed "dances, fancy-dress parties, amateur theatricals, cricket week-ends, gymkhanas, and polo weeks, as well as private supper parties, with their endless rounds of *toasties,* and small *chop,* and weekends luncheon parties," said a former resident.

By its very definition, the club was exclusive in membership. Strict divisions separated those who pursued commercial activities from civil servants, for example, and hierarchies were preserved more fiercely than at home. Tradition and cultural identity seemed especially important to those stationed in the exotic outposts of the Empire, and they pursued their sports and leisure activities with vigor. Where geography, climate, and local culture demanded adaptation, the club accommodated as necessary, creating a hybrid of colonial custom that allowed new worlds to be explored

PRECEDING PAGES *At Ooty, silver trophies and teapots are proudly displayed.*

OPPOSITE *In the Bombay Yacht Club, a hallway is cooled by overhead fans.*

ABOVE *Tea planters who lived outside of town on foothill plantations like this one used their clubs as a home base for visits.*

RIGHT *Planters had their own clubs; a rice plantation owner in Kerala had more in common with farmers than with a military major or civil servant.*

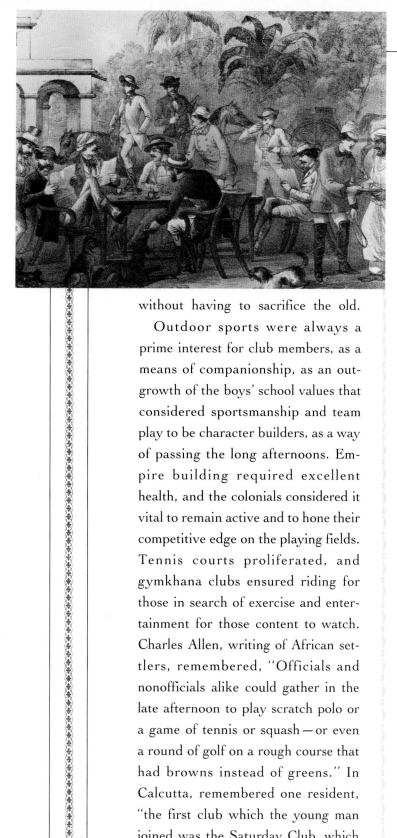

PRECEDING PAGES *Conviviality in the clubhouse was the rule, except in the quiet precincts of the library. Books and magazines would be ordered from England, and usually kept behind glass to protect them from the elements. Although cane was more practical in the tropics, comfortable leather armchairs were a part of the setting.*

ABOVE LEFT *In the early days of colonial rule, life was more informal; men relaxed under banana trees, a drink at the ready.*

ABOVE *Nearly a half-century after independence, time seems to have stood still in the clubs of India.*

OPPOSITE *Dinner is still served under the gaze of winning horses and riders of the past.*

without having to sacrifice the old.

Outdoor sports were always a prime interest for club members, as a means of companionship, as an outgrowth of the boys' school values that considered sportsmanship and team play to be character builders, as a way of passing the long afternoons. Empire building required excellent health, and the colonials considered it vital to remain active and to hone their competitive edge on the playing fields. Tennis courts proliferated, and gymkhana clubs ensured riding for those in search of exercise and entertainment for those content to watch. Charles Allen, writing of African settlers, remembered, "Officials and nonofficials alike could gather in the late afternoon to play scratch polo or a game of tennis or squash — or even a round of golf on a rough course that had browns instead of greens." In Calcutta, remembered one resident, "the first club which the young man joined was the Saturday Club, which

was a social club for dancing and squash and swimming and a generally active social life. Next there was the Tollygunge Club on the outskirts of Calcutta, a very select club with a six year waiting list, which had a golf course, a racecourse and a swimming pool. . . . Then, when a young man got more senior there was the Bengal Club, which was famous for its cuisine and was quite a landmark."

But it was at the close of day that the club reigned, for it was here that men and women spent the twilight, calling for their whiskies and gins. Many men called the club home, since they were alone, by choice or neces-

OPPOSITE *An old-fashioned weighing scale sits by a writing table, where men caught up with their accounts.*

ABOVE *Planters in India wore this distinctive broadbrimmed straw hat.*

sity. Some were forbidden to marry until they had spent a certain number of years in service; others became temporary bachelors when their wives returned to England to settle children in school or visit relatives. Drinking together in the club was better than drinking alone on one's verandah. "Drink became a very necessary part of the day — not drink itself, but

## POLO

Although opinions differ on the origin of polo, many historians believe that the hill tribes of India played a similar game on horseback, tossing a bundle of skins with long lances, to improve their horsemanship for war. The game in its more formal incarnation became identified with British men in the colonies. Many second sons of established families who had a traditional upper-class background but straitened means found that serving in the Army or living in the colonies enabled them to run the expensive string of ponies the game required. The Victorians' regard for vigorous sport encouraged them to head for the polo grounds even when the sun was high. Polo became the occasion for social life, since the earliest clubs were often polo clubs, founded to keep the field and provide a simple clubhouse with its all-important bar, where players and spectators gathered after a game.

seeing one's friends, and relaxing together, and talking of what had gone
on in the office, and what the problems were and such. There was always someone congenial to pass the
time with, and then one could nip
home and have a bath and go to bed
after a late supper, when the house
had cooled," said a former resident of
Malaya.

Other activities offered to club
members were simple — the library
held newspapers and books; card
playing had its partisans, with bridge
a favorite; and, always, there was gos-
sip — trivial or scandalous. In the
Madras Club women were forbidden
to enter the bar and gathered instead
in a special area called the *moorghi-
Khani,* or henhouse. Women circled a
cane table in their basket chairs and
talked for hours of politics, servant
problems, children, or the day's winners at tennis.

The daily round was frequently in-
terrupted by balls and competitions
and race weeks, when members and
guests would dress, and the full pan-

LEFT *The assembly room of the
Delhi Gymkhana Club was once the
scene of fancy dress balls.*

INSET *A porter in his traditional
uniform and turban still welcomes
members to the Gymkhana Club.*

oply of ceremonial colonial life would be unfurled. At Sargodha's race week in the 1930s, the governor of Punjab and the commissioner "drove down the race course in an open carriage with four horses, and all the ladies turned out for the opening in flowered chiffon dresses, hats and gloves, and the men in morning coats," Jennifer Brennan remembers. During the gala celebration afterward at the club, the governor's lady wandered into the exclusively male bar and caused a stir as she lifted her glass.

Visiting club members had large marquees erected at the racecourse for week-long fair weeks. As at home at Ascot, luncheons and parties took place underneath enormous tents, where liveried attendants served grouse stuffed with pâté or chicken in aspic; the tea tents laid on the strawberries and cream. Regimental bands filled the air with bright music. In the larger settlements, nearly every Sat-

urday evening ended with a dance, with a weeknight reserved for a tea dance as well. In Victorian times, any dance served as a matchmakers' hunting ground, especially when the newly arrived young unmarried ladies, rudely called the Fishing Fleet, were crimped and crinolined and prepared to fall in love. (Those who failed to

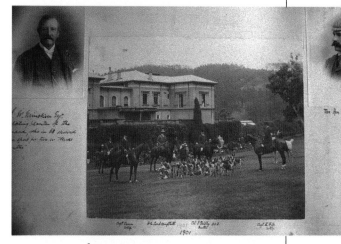

ABOVE *At Ooty, each year was captured in scrapbooks that included menus, programs, and photographs of club activities.*

LEFT *This water buffalo head hangs in the Mount Kenya Safari Club, waystation for many travelers in from the bush.*

OPPOSITE *The men's dressing room at the Willingdon Club in Bombay has all the necessary requirements, including a hatrack and scale.*

H.E. Lord Ampthill (and his three sons)

ABOVE LEFT *Lord Ampthill's sons wore proper riding gear with sola topees.*

ABOVE RIGHT *A nineteenth-century colonial office had classic revolving bookstands.*

LEFT *In the men's dressing room chairs have linen headrests.*

OPPOSITE ABOVE LEFT *Darjeeling tea awaits shipment.*

OPPOSITE ABOVE RIGHT *Women used the club nearly as frequently as men.*

OPPOSITE BELOW LEFT *Ladies order drinks by telephone.*

OPPOSITE BELOW RIGHT *As Prince of Wales, Edward VII stayed in this room.*

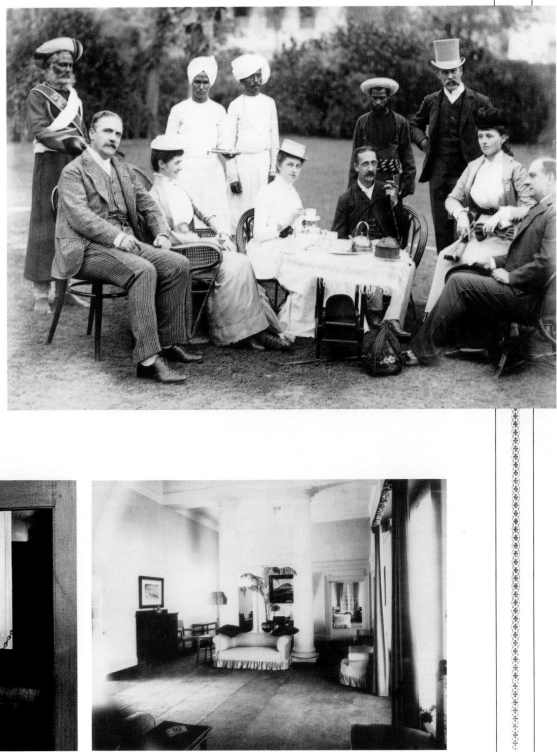

make a match during the season were called the Returned Empties as they sailed home.)

Until the late nineteenth century, most clubhouses differed only in size from the bungalows that housed the clubs' members. By the early twentieth century, even the smallest clubhouses accommodated a range of activities. Jennifer Brennan remembered the club that centered the settlement at Sargodha in Punjab, where,

OPPOSITE *Some clubs had a ladies' bar, men's bar, and mixed bar.*

BELOW *The bulletin board, as this one in the Willingdon Club, served as a message center.*

## GIN, TONIC, AND OTHER DRINKS

Nearly as important as tea in the daily ritual was that more powerful drink taken before lunch or at sundown, whether on one's own verandah or at the club. Drinking spirits had always been an important part of social life; in the eighteenth century a punch was stirred up in a large bowl for convivial assemblies — *punch* itself is a Hindi word. Later on, whisky and gin were the established favorites. A tot of whisky was thought to be reviving; a handclap or a shout summoned the waiter, who would bring a *burra* or *chota* (big or little) peg of whisky, depending on how much reviving was required. And the gin and tonic became a mainstay, especially prized for the medicinal overtones of the quinine in the tonic water. This drink evolved from the constant concern about malaria and the regular regimen of quinine used to treat it. To make the quinine drinkable, sugar and lime or lemon were added — as well as some gin. Called Indian tonic, the concoction was patented in 1858 by Erasmus Bond.

in 1926, twenty-six British families resided: "The club house was a large, low building of red brick with very deep verandas in front and on one side. The verandas were protected by cane *chicks* (blinds) lined with navy-blue canvas to keep out the glare. In the winter the *chicks* were let down and laced together like tents to provide sitting-out room for dances. For those occasions, dhurries were put on the floor, and the verandas decorated with vases of flowers. Little charcoal stoves were scattered around."

At the zenith of colonial power, some clubhouses — especially in major cities like Bombay and Calcutta — were as grand as palaces, with stately architecture, lavishly decorated halls,

PRECEDING PAGES *The Royal Asiatic Society dates to the early days of British settlement in India; its library was both a retreat and an important resource for the community — as it is today.*

OPPOSITE *In the men's bar at Ooty, gentlemen took their ease at the end of the day with a sundowner.*

ABOVE *Basket chairs at the Willingdon Club could be easily arranged for a conversation.*

BELOW LEFT *The provisions made for women's pursuits at the Willingdon Club included a mixed bar and a card room, which would have been busy every afternoon.*

and tall pillars, high ceilings, and costly woods. By the 1940s, especially during World War II, when Indian regiments served beside the rest of the Empire's troops, clubs began to open to prominent members of the native community, too.

The Ootacamund Club, convened in 1843, in the town known as "snooty Ooty," was the premier among clubs at the summer hill stations. Pleasant dining rooms, a welcoming bar, rooms for card playing and billiards (one oft-

repeated legend has Neville Chamberlain perfecting his invention of the game of snooker here as a young subaltern) made the Ootacamund the place where dreams of England could

ABOVE *The Planters' Club in Darjeeling was the center for owners of tea plantations.*

OPPOSITE *The verandah of the Planters' Club looked out on the club's gardens and the hills beyond.*

PRECEDING PAGES *Dinner menu at Ooty Club still includes roast beef and Yorkshire pudding.*

OPPOSITE *The cricket grounds can be seen from the verandah of the Bombay Gymkhana Club.*

ABOVE LEFT *Dinner goers autographed the menu of a 1923 dinner at the Royal Bombay Yacht Club.*

ABOVE RIGHT *Framed views of the Nilgiri Hills and their tea gardens decorate the Ooty walls.*

be most convincingly lived, especially when the air was bracing and rain pattered on the roof. The building began as a hotel built for Sir William Rumbold in 1830 in Neoclassical style, with Ionic columns and a pedimented roof. The club still operates, with native Indian membership. Hunting prints and stuffed trophies still cover its walls, baked fish and lemon tart are still the staples on the menu in its dining room, and diligent servants keep its brass and silver shiny, as if the memsahibs and their husbands had stepped away for only a moment.

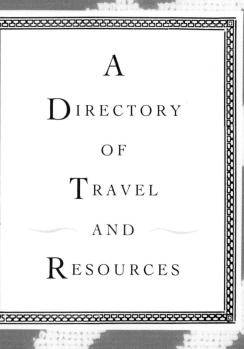

A Directory

OF

Travel

AND

Resources

## Africa

### SAFARIS

ABERCROMBIE & KENT
1520 Kensington Road
Suite 212
Oak Brook, IL 60521
(800) 323-7308

COX & KINGS
511 Lexington Avenue
New York, NY 10017
(212) 935-3935

HEMINGWAY SAFARIS
1050 Second Avenue
New York, NY 10022
(212) 838-3650
Contact: Brian Gainesford

INTO AFRICA, INC.
Lynn Glenn
93 Doubling Road
Greenwich, CT 06830
(203) 869-8165

KER & DOWNEY, INC.
13201 Northwest Freeway
Suite 800
Houston, TX 77040
(800) 231-6352

KER & DOWNEY
SAFARIS LTD./
BILL WINTER SAFARIS
P.O. Box 24871
Nairobi, Kenya
(254) (2) 082146

KER DOWNEY SELBY
P.O. Box 40
Maun, Botswana
(267) 660-211

MICATO SAFARIS
P.O. Drawer 43374
Nairobi, Kenya
(254) (2) 336138
    or
15 West 26th Street
New York, NY 10010
(212) 545-7111
or (800) MICATO-1

ROBIN HURT SAFARIS
LTD.
P.O. Box 24988
Karen, Nairobi, Kenya
(254) (2) 882826

SAFARI RATING
SERVICE
D. H. Doelker
301 East 63rd Street, Suite 17G
New York, NY 10021
(212) 888-7596
or (800) 882-5557

### HOTELS

GIRAFFE MANOR
(Country House Hotel)
Box 15004
Nairobi, Kenya
(254) (2) 891078

MT. KENYA SAFARI
CLUB
P.O. Box 35
Nanyuki, Kenya
(254) (176) 22960

NORFOLK HOTEL
P.O. Box 40064
Nairobi, Kenya
(254) (2) 335422

TREETOPS HOTEL
P.O. Box 23
Nyeri, Kenya
Reservations through Block
Hotels
P.O. Box 47557
Nairobi, Kenya
(254) 335807

VICTORIA FALLS
HOTEL
P.O. Box 10
Victoria Falls, Zimbabwe
(263) (13) 4203/4/5

### PLACES
### OF INTEREST

DURBAR HALL
Osborne House
Cowes
Isle of Wight, England
0983852484

KAREN BLIXEN
MUSEUM
Karen Road (next to Karen
College)
Karen, Nairobi, Kenya
(254) (2) 882 779

KEDLESTON HALL
Indian Museum — Lord Curzon,
Viceroy of India (1899–1905)
Derbyshire
Derby, England
0332842191

KIAMBETHU TEA FARM
Tigoni (22 miles northeast of
Nairobi)
Kenya, Africa
(254) (154) 40756
Mrs. Mitchell

NEHRU GALLERY OF
INDIAN ART
(1550–1900)
Victoria & Albert Museum
Cromwell Road
London, SW1, England
71 9388500

## India

### TRAVEL

OUR PERSONAL GUEST
20 East 53rd St.
New York, NY 10022
(212) 319-4521
Contact: Pallavi Shah or Anita
Trehan
Custom, luxury travel to India

BRITISH AIRWAYS
245 Park Ave.
New York, NY 10017
(800) 247-9297

## Anglo-Indian
## Restaurants

### ENGLAND

CHUTNEY MARY
535 Kings Road
London, SW 10, England
(071) 3513113

### UNITED STATES

BOMBAY CLUB
815 Connecticut Avenue N.W.
Washington. DC
(202) 659-3727

CHAIWALLAH TEA
ROOM
*1 Main Street*
*Salisbury, CT 06068*
*(203) 435-9758*

RANGOON RACQUET
CLUB
*9474 Santa Monica Boulevard*
*Los Angeles, CA*
*(213) 274-8926*

## BERMUDA

BOMBAY BICYCLE
CLUB
*75 Reid Street*
*Bermuda*
*(809) 292-0048*

## MALAYSIA

YE OLDE
SMOKEHOUSE
*Cameron Highlands*
*Malaysia*
*(60) 05941214*

*Sources for
British
Colonial
Furnishings,
Accessories,
and Clothing*

## UNITED STATES

AMERICAN HERITAGE
SHUTTERS
*2345 Dunn Avenue*
*Memphis, TN 38114*
*(901) 743-2800*
*Custom exterior and interior
shutters, functional with
authentic hardware*

ANTIQUE &
DECORATIVE TEXTILE
GALLERY
*254 W. 73rd Street*
*New York, NY 10025*
*(212) 787-0090*
*Paisley shawl collection*
*Contact: Frank Ames*

BALL AND BALL
HISTORIC LIGHTING
*463 West Lincoln Highway*
*Exton, PA 19341*
*(215) 363-7330*
*Reproduction lighting fixtures*

BOMBAY COMPANY
*(800) 829-7789*
*Call for nearest store or mail
order information.*
*Furnishings, decorative
accessories*

BRITISH KHAKI
*214 West 39th Street*
*New York, NY 10018*
*(212) 221-1199*
*Contact: Robert Lighton*
*Safari clothing and accessories*

THE CHELSEA
CATALOG
*1 Chelsea Court*
*Church Hill, MD 21690*
*(800) 866-6464*
*Teak steamer chairs.*

CHINOISERIE
*500 East Lionshead Circle*
*Vail, CO 81657*
*(303) 476-8716*
*Contact: Sara Schmidt Austin*
*Antique furniture and accessories*

CORA GINSBURG
*19 East 74th Street*
*New York, NY 10021*
*(212) 744-1352*
*18th- and 19th-century antique
textiles*

CRESCENT ANTIQUES
*455 West 23rd Street, Suite 17E*
*New York, NY 10011*
*(212) 627-2935 (by
appointment)*
*18th- and 19th-century antique
furniture and home accessories*

GHURKA
*41 East 57th Street*
*New York, NY*
*(212) 826-8300*
*Luggage and accessories*

HARRINGTONS
*East Montauk Highway*
*Southampton, NY 11968*
*(516) 728-0449*
*Raj furniture from Sri Lanka*

HUNTING WORLD
*16 East 53rd Street*
*New York, NY 10022*
*(212) 755-3400*

INDIES LANDING
*Ivanhoe Row*
*1223 North Orange Avenue*
*Orlando, FL 32804*
*(407) 894-0178*
*Fabric, furnishings, antiques*

INDIGO SEAS
*123 North Robertson Street*
*Los Angeles, CA 90048*
*(213) 550-8758*
*Decorative accessories*

THE J. PETERMAN
COMPANY
*2444 Palumbo Drive*
*Lexington, KY 40503*
*(800) 231-7341*
*Mail-order safari
clothes and accessories*

KAMDIN DESIGNS
*791 Lexington Avenue*
*New York, NY 10021*
*(212) 371-8833*
*Indian rugs: sisal and dhurries*

KATIE RIDDER HOME
FURNISHINGS
*944 Lexington Avenue*
*New York, NY 10022*
*(212) 861-2345*
*Colonial furniture, rugs, and
decorative accessories*

MOMBASA CANOPIES
YUNGJOHANN
HILLMAN COMPANY
*2345 Fort Worth Street*
*Grand Prairie, TX 75050*
*(214) 641-5844*
*Mosquito netting*

PRICE-GLOVER
*59 East 79th Street*
*New York, NY 10021*
*(212) 772-1740*
*Antique and reproduction
furniture and decorative
accessories*

RALPH LAUREN
HOME COLLECTION
*1185 Avenue of the Americas*
*New York, NY 10036*
*(212) 642-8700*
*Call for nearest store*
*Safari collection*

**SAFARI OUTFITTERS,
LTD.**
*71 Ethan Allen Highway
Ridgefield, CT 06877
(203) 544-9505
Safari gear*

**WILLIS & GEIGER**
*36 West 44th Street
New York, NY 10036
(212) 764-0808
Safari outfitters*

**VAN RAMPELBURG**
*Box 18474
Nairobi, Kenya
(254) (2) 55 7629
Reproduction steamer chairs*

## INDIA

**CHOR BAZAAR**
*Thieves Market
Mutton Street
Bombay, India
Antiques and accessories*

**SANDRA LONG**
*18 East 33rd Street, #4F
New York, NY 10016
(212) 689-3457
(by appointment)
Anglo-Raj antiques*

**SANYU DESAI**
*(203) 853-9225
(by appointment)
Anglo-Indian furniture*

**SCOTT WARSHAW
COLLECTION**
*7655 Enterprise Drive
Riviera Beach, FL 33404
(407) 844-2325
Painted furniture and accessories*

**THE SHUTTER SHOP**
*P.O. Box 11882
Charlotte, NC 28220-1882
(704) 334-8051
Customizer of interior shutters*

**TAGANDA TEA**
*St. James Holdings, Inc.,
Importers
Box 1212
Natchitoches, LA 71458
(318) 352-4656
Contact: John Robinson
Mail-order African tea*

**WINDOW MODES,
LTD.**
*979 Third Avenue
New York, NY 10022
(212) 752-1140
Custom shutters*

## AFRICA

**AFRICAN HERITAGE**
*Kenyatta Avenue
Nairobi, Kenya
(254) (2) 333157 or (254) (2)
554378*

**ANTIQUITY SHOP**
*Hilton Arcade/Watali Street
(off Mama Ngina Street)
Nairobi, Kenya
(254) (2) 335095*

**INDIAN MERCANTILE
MANSIONS**
*Madame Cama Road
Bombay 400039
India
2020564*

**MAHENDRA DOSHI**
*Giriraj
201, Walkeshwar Road
Bombay, India 400 006
8229526
Antiques (Indian and Raj)*

**PHILLIPS ANTIQUES**
*Bombay, India*

**SUNDER NAGAR**
*New Delhi, India
Antique market area*

**VICTORIA TECHNICAL
INSTITUTE**
*765 Anna Road
Madras, India 60002
Handcrafted items and textiles*

## ENGLAND

**CHELSEA GARDENER**
*125 Sydney Street
London SW3 6NR, England
(44) (71) 3525656
Reproduction colonial-style
chairs and tables*

**CRUCIAL TRADING,
LTD.**
*77 Westbourne Park Road
London W2, England
(44) (71) 2219000
Coir, sisal, and sea grass rugs*

**GLOBAL VILLAGE
CRAFTS, LTD.**
*Sparrow Works, Bower Hinton,
Martock
Somerset, England TZ12 6LG
(44) 935823390
Furnishings and decorative
accessories.*

**JANE TENNANT**
*44 Burlington Gardens
London W3, England
(44) (81) 9929255
Reproduction planter's chairs*

**MUTHAIGA**
*11 Park Street
Stowe-on-the-Wold,
Gloucestershire, England
(44) 4513053
Country house goods from Kenya*

# Glossary

AFGHAN: Woven shawl sometimes worn over other clothing; more commonly used as a small blanket

BANDANNA: Large cotton handkerchief with white pattern on colored ground using classic Upper Indian dyeing technique

BANGLE: Simple circular bracelet, originally made of colored glass, now in silver, gold, wood, or papier-mâché

BAZAAR: Open-air market selling miscellaneous items in small booths or shops

BUNGALOW: Small house, usually one-storied, surrounded by a verandah; derived from the Bengali word *bunglalo* or the Hindi word *bangla*

CALICO: Plain, woven cloth, usually with printed figured pattern

CASHMERE: Anglicized version of fine, soft wool fabric woven from hair of goats raised in Kashmir

CHAI: Indian tea

CHARPOY: Low Indian bed with wood frame and webbing

CHINTZ: Glazed printed cotton fabric, originally inexpensive

CHOTA HAZRI: "Little tea"; tea served before breakfast

COIR: Fiber from coconut husk used to weave rugs and floor mats

DHURRIE: Woven cotton rug

DUNGAREES: Blue denim jeans or overalls; from the Hindi word for coarse fabric

GYMKHANA: Sports meeting; often refers to a riding club

HILL STATION: Village in the mountains in India, such as Simla and Ooty, where British government officers and civilians encamped during hot weather

JUNGLE: "Wilderness"

KHAKI: "Dusty"; used to describe a sturdy cotton twill cloth in this earth color

MADRAS: Woven cotton fabric with large, colorful plaid; originally from the city of this name

MEMSAHIB: Lady (from madam-sahib)

MUFTI: Civilian clothes

MUSLIN: Inexpensive plain-woven cotton made in India, although derivation is Persian

PAISLEY: Stylized pine-nut design woven into or printed on fabric; shawl or scarf made of this fabric

PAJAMAS: Loose drawstring pants worn in the Orient; now common for nightclothes of similar design

PITH HELMET: Sola topee or light cotton fiber-covered helmet

POSH: Port Out, Starboard Home: Seasoned travelers to the colonies knew to book a ship's cabin this way to enjoy the most breeze, least sun and heat

RAJ: Kingdom

RAJAH: Ruler

RATTAN: Long solid-core vine split or peeled and used in constructing lightweight furniture or for caning seats and benches

RED TAPE: Red cloth tape used to tie bundles of documents in India; now common for "unnecessary paperwork"

SAFARI: Swahili for "journey"; long expedition for hunting or exploring

SAHIB: Sir (form used by Indians addressing Europeans)

SALAAM: Salutation of respect

SARI: Indian woman's dress

SUNDOWNER: First drink at sundown in the colonies

TIFFIN: Lunch in the British colonies

VERANDAH: Open, pillared gallery around a home, used as outdoor living space

WALLAH: Man

ZENANA: Indian women's private quarters

# BIBLIOGRAPHY
## NONFICTION

**Aitken, Rhona.** *The Memsahib's Cookbook.*
London: Platkus, 1990.

**Alexander, Caroline.** *One Dry Season: In the Footsteps of Mary Kingsley.* New York:
Alfred A. Knopf, 1990.

**Allen, Charles.** *A Glimpse of the Burning Plain: Letters from the India Journals of Charlotte Canning.* London: Michael
Joseph, 1986.

————. *Plain Tales from the Raj.* New York:
Holt, Rinehart & Winston, 1985.

————. *Tales from the Dark Continent: Images of British Colonial Africa in the Twentieth Century.* London: Futura Publications,
1979.

————. *Tales from the South China Seas: Images of the British in South-East Asia in the Twentieth Century.* London: Futura Publications,
1983.

**Ames, Frank.** *The Kashmir Shawl.*
Woodbridge, England: Antique Collectors
Club, 1988.

**Batchelor, John and Julie.** *In Stanley's Footsteps.* London: Blandford, 1990.

**Beard, Peter.** *The End of the Game: The Last Word from Paradise.* New York: Chronicle
Books, 1988.

**Bierman, John.** *Dark Safari: The Life Behind the Legend of Henry Morton Stanley.*
New York: Alfred A. Knopf, 1990.

**Brennan, Jennifer.** *Curries & Bugles: A Cookbook of the British Raj.* London:
Viking, 1990.

**Bull, Bartle.** *Safari: A Chronicle of Adventure.* New York: Viking, 1988.

*Calcutta: Changing Visions, Lasting Images Through 300 Years.* Bombay: Marg
Publications, 1990.

**Cowasjee, Saros.** *Stories from the Raj: From Kipling to Independence.* London: The Bodley
Head, 1982.

**Davies, Philip.** *Splendors of the Raj: British Architecture in India 1660–1947.* New York:
Viking Penguin, 1987.

**Dinesen, Isak.** *Letters from Africa: 1914–1931.* Chicago: University of Chicago Press, 1981.

————. *Out of Africa.* New York: Random
House, 1984.

**Eden, Emily.** *Up the Country: Letters from India.* London: Virago Press, 1983.

**Farwell, Byron.** *The Gurkhas.* New York:
Viking, 1990.

**Fay, Eliza.** *Original Letters from India (1779–1815).* London: Hogart, 1986.

**Fowler, Marian.** *Below the Peacock Fan.*
New York: Viking Penguin, 1987.

Ganesan, Indira. *The Journey*. New York: Alfred A. Knopf, 1990.

Goodwin, Jason. *The Gun Powder Gardens: Travels Through India and China in Search of Tea*. London: Chatto and Windus, 1990.

Head, Raymond. *The Indian Style*. Chicago: The University of Chicago Press, 1986.

Heminway, John Hyman. *No Man's Land: A Personal Journey into Africa*. New York: Dutton, 1983.

Hibbert, Christopher. *Africa Explored: Europeans in the Dark Continent 1769–1889*. New York: W. W. Norton, 1982.

Irving, Robert Grant. *Indian Summer: Wryens, Baker and Imperial Delhi*. New Haven: Yale University Press, 1984.

Jacob, Violet. *Diaries and Letters from India 1895–1900*. Edinburgh: Canongate Publishing, 1990.

Kaye, M. M. *The Golden Calm: An English Lady's Life in Moghul Delhi*. Exeter, England: Webb and Bower, 1980.

————. *The Sun in the Morning: My Early Years in India and England*. New York: St. Martin's Press, 1990.

Kusoom, Vadgama. *India in Britain: The Indian Contribution to the British Way of Life*. London: Robert Royce, Ltd., 1984.

Lauren, Ricky. *Safari*. New York: Polo-Ralph Lauren, 1989.

Lovell, Mary S. *Straight on Till Morning: A Biography of Beryl Markham*. New York: St. Martin's Press, 1987.

MacMillan, Margaret. *Women of the Raj*. London: Thames and Hudson, 1988.

Markham, Beryl. *West with the Night*. North Point Press, 1983.

Morris, James. *Pax Britannica: The Climax of an Empire*. New York: Harcourt Brace Jovanovich, 1968.

Naipaul, V. S. *India: A Million Mutinies Now*. New York: Viking, 1991.

Nehru, Jawaharlal. *The Discovery of India*. New York: Anchor Books, 1990.

Permor-Hesketh, Robert. *Architecture of the British Empire*. New York: The Vendome Press, 1986.

Potter, Jennifer. *Long Lost Journey*. San Francisco: Mercury House, 1990.

Ricciardi, Mirella. *Vanishing Africa*. New York: Holt, Rinehart & Winston, 1977.

Rice, Edward. *Captain Sir Richard Francis Burton*. New York: Charles Scribner's Sons, 1990.

Roosevelt, Theodore. *African Game Trails*. New York: Charles Scribner's Sons, 1910.

Swayne-Thomas, April. *Indian Summer: A Mem-Sahib in India and Sind*. London: New English Library, 1981.

*The Raj: India and the British 1600–1947*. London: National Portrait Galleries Publications, 1990.

Theroux, Paul. *The Imperial Way*. Boston: Houghton Mifflin, 1985.

Thurman, Judith. *Isak Dinesen: The Life of a Story Teller*. New York: St. Martin's Press, 1982.

Trevelyan, Raleigh. *The Golden Oriole: A 200-Year History of an English Family in India.* New York: Touchstone, 1987.

Victoria and Albert Museum. *Indian Architectural Designs.* New York: Harry N. Abrams, 1989.

\*\*Viney, Graham. *The Colonial Houses of South Africa.* London: New Holland Publishers.

Wilson, Lady. *Letters from India (1889–1905).* London: Century Classics, 1989.

Worswick, Clark, and Ainslee Embree. *The Last Empire: Photographs in British India 1855–1911.* New York: Aperture, 1990.

Yule, Col. Henry and A. C. Burnell. *Hobson-Jobson: A Glossary of Colloquial Anglo-Indian Words and Phrases.* Calcutta: Rupa and Co., 1986.

# FICTION

Barlow, Linda. *Leaves of Fortune.* New York: Dell, 1990.

Courter, Gay. *Flowers in the Blood.* New York: Dutton, 1990.

Forster, E. M. *A Passage to India.* New York: Buccaneer Books, 1981.

Fosburgh, Lacey. *India Gate.* New York: Crown, 1991.

Godden, Rumer. *Black Narcissus.* New York: Viking Penguin, 1939.

————. *Kingfishers Catch Fire.* New York: Viking Penguin, 1955.

————. *A Time to Dance, No Time to Weep.* Anstey, England: F. A. Thorpe, 1989.

————. *The Green Gage Summer.* New York: Viking Penguin, 1958.

————. *The Peacock Spring.* New York: Viking Penguin, 1975.

————. *The River.* New York: Viking Penguin, 1946.

————. *Two Under the Indian Sun.* New York: Viking Penguin, 1966.

Huxley, Elspeth. *Flame Trees of Thika.* London: Penguin Books, 1959.

————. *Livingstone and His African Journeys.* London: Penguin Books, 1974.

————. *Nellie: Letters from Africa.* London: Penguin Books, 1980.

————. *Out in the Mid-Day Sun: My Kenya.* London: Penguin Books, 1985.

————. *The Challenge of Africa.* London: Penguin Books, 1971.

————. *The Mottled Lizard.* London: Penguin Books, 1982.

Jhabvala, Ruth Prawer. *Heat and Dust.* New York: Harper and Row, 1976.

Kaye, M. M. *Shadow of the Moon.* New York: Bantam, 1980.

————. *The Far Pavilions.* New York: St. Martin's Press, 1978.

Kipling, Rudyard. *The Man Who Would Be King.* New York: Oxford University Press, 1987.

————. *Kim.* New York: Oxford University Press, 1987.

————. *The Jungle Book.* New York: Oxford University Press, 1987.

———. *Plain Tales from the Hills.* New York: Viking, 1987.

**Maugham, W. Somerset.** *The Letter: A Play in Three Acts.* Salem: Ayer, 1977.

———. *Collected Short Stories, Volume 1.* New York: Viking Penguin, 1977.

———. *Collected Short Stories, Volume 2.* New York: Viking Penguin, 1991.

———. *Collected Short Stories, Volume 4.* New York: Viking Penguin, 1978.

**Mehta, Gita.** *Raj.* New York: Simon and Schuster, 1989.

**Scott, Paul.** *Staying On.* New York: Avon Books, 1979.

———. *The Raj Quartet: The Jewel in the Crown; The Day of the Scorpion; The Towers of Silence; A Division of the Spoils.* New York: Avon Books, 1979.

# FILMOGRAPHY

*The African Queen*
*Autobiography of a Princess*
*Beyond the Blue Horizon*
*Black Narcissus*
*Born Free*
*Cheetah*
*China Seas*
*Clive of India*
*Coup de Torchon*
*Daktari*
*The Deceivers*
*Elephant Walk*
*End of the Empire*
*The Far Pavilions*

*The Four Feathers*
*Gandhi*
*Gorillas in the Mist*
*Gunga Din*
*Hatari*
*Heat and Dust*
*The Householders*
*Kim*
*King Solomon's Mines*
*The Kitchen Toto*
*The Last Viceroy*
*Lawrence of Arabia*
*The Letter*
*The Little Princess*
*The Lives of a Bengal Lancer*
*Lost Horizon*
*The Man Who Would Be King*
*Mogambo*
*Mr. Johnson*
*The Music Room*
*Out of Africa*
*A Passage to India*
*Queenie*
*The Rains Came*
*The Rains of Ranchipur*
*Red Dust*
*Rogue's March*
*Shadow of the Sun*
*Shakespeare Wallah*
*The Snows of Kilimanjaro*
*Stanley and Livingstone*
*Staying On*
*They Met in Bombay*
*Tradewinds*
*Valley of the Kings*
*Wee Willie Winkie*
*White Hunter, Black Heart*

# Notes

p. 13  "The Empire builder's jargon..." Roald Dahl, *Going Solo* (Penguin, 1986), p. 3.

p. 15  "By dint of hanging up..." Margaret MacMillan, *Women of the Raj* (Thames and Hudson, 1988), p. 45.

p. 15  "Empires come, empires go..." Jan Morris, quoted in Charles Allen's *Architecture of the British Empire* (The Vendome Press, 1986), p. 11.

p. 17  "Suddenly a puff of wind..." Joseph Conrad, quoted in Charles Allen's *Tales from the South China Seas* (Futura, 1983), p. 19.

p. 18  "Messrs. Silver & Co.,..." An advertisement quoted in Charles Allen's *Tales from the Dark Continent* (Futura, 1979), p. 16.

p. 23  "The cabin was inviting..." Rumer Godden, *Two Under the Indian Sun* (William Morrow and Company, 1966), p. 12.

p. 35  "The first impression..." Charles Allen, *A Glimpse of the Burning Plain* (London: Michael Joseph, 1986).

p. 39  "a camp chair, a camp stool..." Charles Meek, quoted in Charles Allen's *Tales from the Dark Continent* (Futura, 1979), p. 34.

p. 39  "touring was conducted..." Charles Allen, *Plain Tales from the Raj* (Holt, Rinehart and Winston, 1985).

p. 40  "Inside each tent were our beds..." Emily Eden, *Up the Country* (Virago, 1983), p. 23.

p. 45  "The string of 28 camels left..." Lady Wilson, *Letters from India* (Century, 1989) p. 1.

p. 45  "Anything cosier than our tent..." Lady Wilson, *Letters from India* (Century, 1989) p. 13.

p. 46  "This play takes its name..." George Otto as quoted by Raleigh Trevelyan's *The Oriole* (A Touchstone Book, Simon & Schuster, 1987), p. 419.

p. 51  "There was not much choice..." Harriet Tytler, *An Englishwoman in India: The Memoirs of Harriet Tytler, 1828–58.*

p. 52  "When you arrived..." Jennifer Brennan, *Curries & Bugles* (HarperCollins Publishers, 1990), pp. 149–50.

p. 54  "We are but birds of..." Lady Wilson, *Letters from India* (Century, 1989), p. 6.

p. 67  "Most of the houses were one-storeyed..." B. L. Clay, quoted in Charles Allen's *Architecture of the British Empire*, p. 70.

p. 68  "of one storey..." Charles Allen, *Architecture of the British Empire*, p. 58.

p. 74  "burst into a tent of white blossom..." Rumer Godden, *Two Under the Indian Sun* (Viking Penguin, 1966), p. 25.

p. 85  "the ceilings were high..." Margaret MacMillan, *Women of the Raj* (Thames and Hudson, 1988), p. 76.

p. 85  "It is so very HOT..." Emily Eden, *Up the Country*, p. 268.

p. 89  "The fuss of punkahs..." Charles Allen, *A Glimpse of the Burning Plain*, p. 19.

p. 92  "We wanted a long bamboo sofa..." Violet Jacob, *Diaries and Letters from India* (Canongate, 1990), p. 32.

p. 94  "The degree of destructiveness of this climate..." Emily Eden, quoted in Marian Fowler's *Below the Peacock Fan* (Penguin, 1987), p. 32.

p. 97  "the land of loll..." Edith Cuthell, quoted in Margaret MacMillan's *Women of the Raj*, p. 78.

p. 99  "The rooms are invariably dark..." Isabel Savory, quoted in Margaret MacMillan's *Women of the Raj*, p. 77.

p. 99  "I am getting so fond of this place..." Charles Allen, *A Glimpse of the Burning Plain*, p. 34.

p. 100  "To us the drawing-room..." Rumer Godden, *Two Under the Indian Sun*, p. 77.

p. 102  "It is provoking..." Charles Allen, *A Glimpse of the Burning Plain*, p. 31.

p. 102  "formidable old lady..." Philip Mason, from the foreword in Charles Allen's *Plain Tales from the Raj*, p. 15.

p. 109  "It was a menu order..." Jennifer Brennan, *Curries & Bugles*, pp. 251–52.

p. 110  "We would inveigh against..." Margaret Macmillan, *Women of the Raj* (Thames and Hudson, 1988), p. 69.

p. 119  "A lot of fun..." Charles Allen, *Plain Tales from the Raj*, p. 116.

p. 123  "dances, fancy-dress parties..." Charles Allen, *Tales from the Dark Continent*, p. 71.

p. 126  "Officials and nonofficials..." Charles Allen, *Tales from the Dark Continent*, p. 71.

p. 126  "the first club..." Charles Allen, *Plain Tales from the Raj*, p. 119.

p. 131  "drove down the race course..." Jennifer Brennan, *Curries & Bugles*, p. 197.

p. 141  "The club house..." Jennifer Brennan, *Curries & Bugles*, p. 195.

# *Index*